BOGNOR BILL
A Grey County Maverick

RON PEGG

BOGNOR BILL: A GREY COUNTY MAVERICK
Copyright © 2016 by Ron Pegg

All rights reserved. Neither this publication nor any part of this publication may be reproduced or transmitted in any form or by any means, electronic or mechanical, including photocopying, recording or any information storage and retrieval system, without permission in writing from the author.

Printed in Canada

ISBN: 978-1-4866-1316-8

Word Alive Press
131 Cordite Road, Winnipeg, MB R3W 1S1
www.wordalivepress.ca

Library and Archives Canada Cataloguing in Publication

Pegg, Ron, 1938-, author
    Bognor Bill : a Grey County maverick / Ron Pegg.

Issued in print and electronic formats.
ISBN 978-1-4866-1316-8 (paperback).--ISBN 978-1-4866-1317-5 (ebook)

    1. Murdoch, Bill. 2. Ontario. Legislative Assembly--Biography. 3. Legislators--Ontario--Grey (County)--Biography. 4. Politicians--Ontario--Grey (County)--Biography. I. Title.

FC3077.1.M87P44 2016   971.3'04092   C2016-901792-3
    C2016-901793-1

Dedication

This book is dedicated to the memory of Murray Juffs, the principal of Grey Highlands Secondary School in Flesherton during its first fifteen years. Mr. Juffs was a true Maverick.

And to the memory of Jordan Fawcett, who left us much too early.

Christmas is the time to join together and rejoice the birth of Christ. It is also the time to give "Thanks" for what is important to each of us, as in our family, friends an most of all peace in the world. One should take this Holiday Season to say "Thank You" and wish everyone a warm Season`s Greeting.

Myself along with Amanda Brown the 2007 Ontario Miss Mid West Queen, and the 2007 Ontario Little Miss Princess Jordan Fawcett wish to take this time to say "Thank You" for all you have done for the Pageant. It is with business`s and people like yourself that help to make this Pageant successful, and we are truly grateful for your contribution.

On behalf of myself, Amanda and Jordan, we would like to wish you and your family a very Merry Christmas and a Happy New Year. May the memories from this Christmas be with you, your family and friends forever. Again we truly appreciate your contribution to the Ontario Miss and Princess Pageant, again, we "Thank You" and God bless.

Sincerely
Pageant President, Barb MacArthur

Barb MacArthur

2007 Ontario Miss Mid West Queen Amanda Brown

Amanda Brown

2007 Ontario Little Miss Princess, Jordan Fawcett

Jordan Fawcett

Special Thanks to:
Ana Sajfert: Legislative Aide in the constituency office at Queens Park
Bill and Susan Murdoch in spending time with us
and providing many, many, resources.
The Owen Sound constituency office of Bill Walker
Sandra Breedon: Bill's right hand secretary in the Owens Sound and Markdale office from 1990–2011.
Thanks also to the following for being helpful in developing this manuscript:
Wilda Allen: Flesherton Library
Tony Ambrosio
Murray Betts
Bob Clark
Pat Parker Clark
Bob Elliot
Ken MacIntyre
Cathy Murdoch
Fred Wallace

Introduction

During the years that Bill Murdoch was our MPP, we always voted for him. On a number of occasions someone would suggest that we vote for someone else. There were even those times that we had a friend running for one of the other parties. The teachers' federation always wanted to be politically active, and although there were times when it suggested voting Conservative, there were also those times when the pressure was on to vote Liberal or NDP. Whenever there was a community event in the village of Flesherton, Ontario, Bill gave his support. To add to this, his secretary, Sandra, was a former student who was always very efficient and helpful; therefore, when the suggestions came to vote for someone other than Bill, a standard reply was offered: as long as Bill Murdoch is running, he will get my vote. There was never any question.

Having had the opportunity to spend some time with him in the preparation of this book, I have come to understand completely why we always supported Bill.

Bill has a deep love for people, regardless of race, colour, or political persuasion. On the other hand, if he disagrees with a person, he'll certainly let his opinion be known—not as a personal criticism, but as it pertains to the issue being discussed.

In my second book, *The Last of the Small Town Boys,* I claim that I am the last of the small town boys; however, I must concede this title to Bill. He is certainly the last of the small town boys. Although he was born in the Meaford hospital, he has spent almost his entire life in his beloved Bognor, which is the reason for the title of the book. Many people know him as Bognor Bill.

During his time in politics, he always fought for the right of the individual. He always fought for his constituents. He was the champion of the small town. Although he had an interest in many other areas, his first concern was always that of the people in his riding. They had elected him; he represented them.

It is this love of his for the people of small town Ontario that makes Bill and me kindred spirits. He chose the political way. In 1976, I left the elected executive of Ontario Baseball to become its Secretary Manager for the next two decades, where I gained the reputation as the spokesperson for the small towns in Ontario Baseball.

It has been a great pleasure to work on this book.

CHAPTER 1

Getting to Grey County

This chapter has very little to do with Bill directly, but rather describes and provides background on Grey County.

As a small boy in the late 1940s, I lived in a society that really didn't travel much. When we did travel, it was usually to "the known." It was where family was, or where there was a big event like the Brampton or Woodbridge fall fairs.

My first trip to Creemore was to see the final game in a baseball playoff between the Beeton senior team and the senior team from Thornbury. As we travelled from Everett to Creemore, our driver, the Reverend David Gault, pointed out to us the number of times we crossed over the CNR railway track of the branch link that ran from Beeton to Collingwood. The road was so twisty that we crossed over the line twenty two times.

As we were approaching Creemore, I became aware of what were the "mountains" to the west. The big hills were new to me. What was on top of those hills was something to only imagine. I recall having this same recurring thought over the next number of years. I had never been on top of those hills. It was not part of our world. When one went west from Alliston, the world literally stopped at Shelburne. No one from our part of the world ever travelled in that world beyond Shelburne.

The time came that our bantam hockey team featuring Wayne Carleton was playing Mildmay for the Ontario championship. At that time the winner of the Ontario Minor Hockey league would play off against the Western Ontario Athletic Association winner for the championship of Southern Ontario. The WOAA had its headquarters in Wingham, and the Western Ontario Athletic Association refused to become part of the organization that represented the rest of rural southern Ontario. Do we sense a maverick?

A friend of mine, Jimmy McKay, had a son on the team. We drove to Shelburne and then went north to Flesherton. This was early April, and often there was just room for two cars to pass between the six foot snow banks that were on the side of the road. Outside of the fact that Beeton won, the snow banks were my first major memory of Grey County.

It was only a couple of years later that my friend and college roommate, Alex Taylor, asked me to take a summer church service for him. He was the student minister on a charge that included Holstein, Letterbreen, and Varney. On the Saturday night I drove across the road from Shelburne to Mount Forest to spend the night in Holstein at the home of the Aikens—one of the most prominent families in the area.

After preaching on the Sunday with the last service in Varney on the Sunday evening, I drove to Durham and across to Flesherton on my way home. I remember my first thoughts of Flesherton. There were two big buildings on the corner as you turned to go south. The two big buildings gave me the impression that this was a very drab place. By the way, one of the corner buildings was completely destroyed by fire a couple of years later. I never dreamt on that Sunday night that I would be living in Grey County for over half of my life, but I was beginning to get a feeling for what was on top of those hills that I had seen in the distance on my trips to Creemore.

I was just beginning to understand that this was indeed rural country. I was just beginning to understand that this was maverick country. People did their own thing and believed in their deepest heart that they had the right to be free. It is the same spirit that the pioneers of this great nation of Canada had. It is the same spirit that is the heart of Bill Murdoch, and the heart of all true mavericks.

CHAPTER 2

Bognor

There are two kinds of people in this world: those who came from Bognor, and those who wish they did. This is one of the many Bognor sayings called "Bognorisms." Where is Bognor, and what is it about?

As one approaches Grey County on the highways from Collingwood to Owen Sound, they will see a number of signposts indicating that if they take this road, it will lead to Walters Falls. If a person is driving north on Highway 10 to Owen Sound through Grey County, they will see many signposts indicating that if they take this road, it will lead to Walters Falls. What does Walters Falls have to do with Bognor? One needs to look no further than Bill Murdoch to find the answer.

There is the hamlet of Bognor. According to Bill, there is the area surrounding Bognor, which makes up a much larger place. There is Bognor North, Bognor West, East Upper Bognor—where Bill and his wife, Susan, live—and Bognor South. Walters Falls is part of Bognor South. Although a number of the citizens of Walter's Falls claim that their hamlet is not part of Bognor, Mr. Murdoch continues to include the Falls as part of Bognor South. Much of Bognor North is a vast marshland, which is officially called the Bognor Marsh.

The actual hamlet of Bognor is found just south of Highway 26 and just west of Meaford. Due to amalgamation, Bognor is part of Meaford … but don't try telling a lifelong Bognor resident that this is so. They are citizens of Bognor.

Bognor was originally called Sydenham Mills in 1840, but this caused confusion with another Sydenham, especially with incoming mail. A post office had been established in 1873 and the second postmaster, C.H. Heming, renamed Sydenham Mills, Bognor. The name Bognor came from Mr. Heming's family tradition. His father had come from Bognor in England. The little settlement officially became Bognor on June 1, 1879. Today in 2016, Bognor is truly a hamlet. There are fifty-four homes with little construction of new dwellings taking place. There are in the neighbourhood of one hundred fifty registered voters. The post office is very important in the community—the post office where Bill Murdoch's father, Dick, delivered mail to the rural area around Bognor for sixty-five years. There were two churches in Bognor, but after the United Church closed its doors and the Anglican one was demolished in 1981, there are no longer any churches.

The former community centre in which the Murdoch family spent many hours for various community events was destroyed by fire. A new community centre was built across the street from the park where ball and soccer are played.

The names of the streets in the town reflect the age of the growth of the community. John, William, Queen, and Frank are typical street names.

The Women's Institute played a major role in Bognor for over seventy years, beginning in the 1920s. Like most Women's Institutes, however, the one in Bognor lost its significance with the changing times in the life of women.

The only significant business in town is the Grey-Bruce Coatings and Insulation Company, which employs eleven people. It has been the main enterprise of Bill Murdoch's brother-in-law, Gord, for the past forty years. It has its headquarters just over the new bridge on Side Road 6 leading up to East Upper Bognor.

Grey-Bruce Coatings and Insulation serves Grey, Bruce, and Simcoe counties. This company is also the major advertiser on Murdoch's open line radio show on Owen Sound's 560 CFOS, which can be heard on Mondays, Wednesdays, and Fridays from 9:00 a.m. to 10:00 a.m.

The Bognor Marsh in Bognor North is one of the largest marshes in the Grey-Bruce region. It covers 668 hectares and has 119 km of trails. Some of these trails provide access to the famous Bruce Trail, which runs along the Niagara Escarpment. On the brow of the Escarpment, turkey vultures can often be observed as they soar above the hills. But there is no truth to the story that there is a "still" in Bognor North.

This chapter began with a Bognorism. Here are a few more: "He is a so skinny that he has to stand twice to make a shadow," "I like my eggs one beside the other," "It's as handy as a pocket on a shirt," "He tries to dance, but he has a Methodist foot," and "Does a one legged duck swim in circles?" Of course there's a Bognorism about Bill himself: "I'm known as 'Bognor Bill,' and— it could be added— awfully proud of it!" The one-liners only begin to tell the story of the sense of humour that has always been a very important part of Bognor.

One story that was often repeated in Bognor was the story of the horse that was pastured on the side of the hill. The story was written in *The Bognor Chronicle*:

> When we were living up at the Rock, we had a horse that was pastured on the side of the hill. Consequently, the horse grew up with two legs longer than the other two! If you hitched up the horse to a plough, it would just fall over. We decided to take the horse down to the blacksmith and have six inches trimmed from the longer hoofs. What a surprise when we got the horse back and found the blacksmith had trimmed the wrong hoofs. If you hitched it to a plough it would just fall over.

CHAPTER 3

The Murdoch Family

Dick and Betty Murdoch had three children. Billy was the oldest; John, much quieter than Billy, was the second child; and the baby of the family was Elizabeth.

Dick Murdoch was known to every person in Bognor and for miles around. His sixty-five years of delivering the mail to surrounding rural routes meant that his name was known to at least three generations of people in the area. Dick was known to be a quiet gentleman who loved kids.

Dick often took kids, as well as other adults, on his afternoon mail routes. This was primarily for company and enjoyment. During these times a new game developed called

"Slopski, Slopski." While riding in the car, the deal was to collect horse sightings by calling out "slopksi, slopski." The first person to call out the words would receive those horses for their collection. Everyone kept track of how many horses they had called. This went on for some time until someone spotted a graveyard and said, "Bury them all!" This person received everyone's horses and won the game. There would be up to five or six kids in the car, all screaming "slopski, slopski," mostly in Dick's ear. Some of the kids were Elizabeth Murdoch, John Murdoch, Bev Harron, and Larry Harron. Finally, Dick had to do something. It was too noisy even for him. There was no more slopski.

In Dick's younger days, soccer (football) was a big sport in the Bognor area. Bognor had one of the better teams, and Dick was an important member. Dick also enjoyed playing pool in the hamlet's pool hall. This was one sport that young Bill never developed an interest in, because people under eighteen were not allowed in the hall.

Bill's mother, Betty, was a schoolteacher who was very pleased that Bill's brother and sister both became teachers. She said at least once that Bill might have been a very successful teacher if the politicians had only left him alone. This, of course, is a mother talking who was herself a teacher. The Murdoch children had to go two miles to the one room school where they received their public school education.

Bill tells the story of when he was still a very young lad and he and some friends decided to try smoking. He had a hay fort which seemed like a good place in which to experiment. It was a fort that he and his friends had built. They had just started with their experiment when Bill's mother arrived at the fort. She immediately gave young Bill a physical tune up that he's never forgotten. He never tried smoking again. Bill is thankful to this day that his mother caught him— not only because it ended his desire to smoke, but also because his mother probably saved his life, as the hay fort could easily have caught on fire with him inside.

Beside the Murdoch home was an old steam engine that the kids from Bognor liked to play on. It provided many hours of make believe.

By the time Bill and John were old enough to take an interest in sports, soccer was no longer as popular as it once was. The two young boys took up hockey and baseball. The hockey began on the little patches of ice that could be found in the immediate area in the winter. Later on, the boys began playing in the Owen Sound program. Bill would become a member of a juvenile team that won an Ontario championship. John is still playing some old timers hockey. John's greater interest was fastball, and for many years he was a member of outstanding Owen Sound teams that were competitive both provincially and nationally. Bill, in his own right, became an excellent pitcher, but mainly in the local league that Bognor played in.

The Sunday evening meal that Betty prepared each week was a feast that the family always enjoyed. It didn't take the children long to come to appreciate that their mother was an excellent cook.

The Christmas season was another important time for the Murdochs. In Bill's own words:

... being the oldest of three children, I liked to organize. So when we opened our presents Christmas morning, I would put the gifts away ... even the ones that belonged to my brother, John, and my sister, Elizabeth! And if there were toys I wanted to play with, I would ... even if they weren't mine! When you're the oldest, you like to take charge. Days before Christmas, John and I would distract Elizabeth enough (usually asking her to play downstairs) while we looked upstairs for the presents. You see, if Elizabeth knew what we were doing, she'd tell Mom and Dad! We never did find where the presents were. I used to get model cars for Christmas. I could never have enough. I was also into painting when I was younger. Mom and Dad made sure I had all the paint I needed to work on my artist side.

This was written by Bill in 1998. In the conclusion of the article, he goes on to say that he, John, and Elizabeth were still celebrating Christmas morning at their parents' home.

The Murdoch family regularly attended the United Church in Bognor while the children were growing up. When there was a social event at the church, the family usually attended.

Many also were the events that the family attended as a group, or as individuals, at the old community hall. Most of these events involved music. Not only the Murdochs, but many people from Bognor and the surrounding area attended these concerts and dances.

And there was also "Fort Loon."

Dick Murdoch Family Circa 1998

Dick Murdoch Family Circa 1980

CHAPTER 4

An Interlude

Grey County is indeed a land that produces mavericks. Individuality is an important characteristic of the area. Even before Bill got to the provincial legislature in Toronto, there were famous mavericks from Grey. One of these was Eddie Sargent. We can learn much about this maverick from the biography of his life, *Roses in December*, written by his daughter, Patty Belle Sargent.

His daughter relates the story of Eddie's connection with Mr. Howard Fleming, the owner of the *Sun Times* newspaper, which Eddie delivered. Eddie had never met Mr. Fleming personally, but he had heard much about him.

Eddie delivered the paper for two years and had three separate paper routes. He had even recruited two other boys to help him, and they all took a share of the earnings. When Eddie became aware that carriers in other communities were being paid more than him, he went to talk to Mr. Fleming. On the day he went to talk with the publisher, he was told he wouldn't be able to see him.

> Eddie told the man in charge, "How do you do, Mister," as he shook the surprised employer's hand. "My name is Eddie Sargent and I have been a paperboy here for over two years now. I have been a good worker for you, Mister. I always have my collection in on time. I notice I haven't gotten a raise since I started. So I'm asking you to raise my pay to three cents per paper per week." He was quickly ushered out of the office.[1]

Eddie was justifiably upset, and told his dad, Will, about it that night. Will, being a union man, suggested that Eddie organize a strike, so that's exactly what he did.

Eddie rallied his fellow carriers and told them that they were being treated like chumps, as they were doing all the work but management was making all the money. By walking out, the carriers would be showing how essential they were to getting the paper out. On the following Friday all the carriers in Owen Sound went on strike. As they were picketing around the *Sun Times* building, Mr. Fleming came out and demanded to know who was responsible for the unrest:

"I am sir," Eddie said, stepping forward.
"What's your name, boy?" Mr. Fleming asked.
"I'm Eddie Sargent, sir. I organized this." Eddie was proud that he had managed such a coup. He also felt profoundly privileged to be noticed by Mr. Fleming himself. It was a short-lived euphoria.
"You're fired!" were the last words Mr. Fleming said before heading back inside and firmly closing the door behind him.[2]

Years later, Eddie served on city council. In late 1946, about two years into his term, Eddie was approached by a reporter from the *Sun Times* asking if it was true that he'd be running for mayor. The reporter followed up his inquiry with the words: "You're not that stupid, are you?"

That final jab made Eddie mad, and although he'd decided against running for mayor, he now stated that he would run, and even provided the reporter with permission to quote him on that! The story was reported in the paper the next day, which is how Roma, Eddie's wife, got the news. She was understandably upset, as she and Eddie had decided together that he wouldn't run so that he would have more time for family.

The incumbent mayor also got mad. Mayor J. Ernest Knox was part of the Owen Sound establishment and carried great influence with all of the important community leaders. He wasn't concerned about losing the election, but it was generally considered an insult for an incumbent mayor to be challenged by anyone, no matter who it was. When questioned by a reporter the next day, the mayor declared: "Eddie Sargent is nothing but a young up-start." Things went downhill from there:

> At a major public meeting, he attacked Eddie as an incompetent and undesirable candidate. He said Owen Sound would be ruined under his leadership. Eddie, though, didn't want to ruffle the Mayor's feathers any more than he already had—he wanted to make peace. He got up and praised Mr. Knox, saying he was a good man. So Eddie ended up looking like a gentlemen and the mayor ended up looking like a bad sport, even though Eddie said he wasn't.[3]

But Eddie was undeterred:

> Mayor Knox continued to view Eddie as a redneck kid. It was true he was young, but Eddie couldn't remember the last time he felt carefree and innocent or naïve about the world. His demeanor was somewhat fanciful, belying the truth that within Eddie was a very determined man. Now he needed to show the voters he had what it took to do the job and to do it well.[4]

Eddie was excited at the idea of being mayor, and he dreamt of what he could accomplish. As Alderman, he had to defer to senior city officials and the other alderman, but as mayor, he could be even more effective. The election was held, and Eddie became mayor.

In time, Eddie was elected to the Ontario Legislature as the Liberal member for Owen Sound-Grey North. He continued to fight for the underdog, as was evidenced in his very first speech in which he attacked the Ontario Development Agency:

> "Mr. Speaker," he said, "in the Speech from the Throne, The Honourable Prime Minister makes reference to the Ontario

Development Agency. Last spring many of you will remember a loan was made to an Owen Sound industry. The first loan, I believe, made by this newly formed authority. Many of you in this house will recall that in Owen Sound, being aware that his loan—the first of its kind under the New Act—was forthcoming, we were informed that it was a highly secret matter until the announcement was made in the House by the Minister. With great fanfare the announcement was made—and, to be perfectly frank, gentlemen, regardless of who received the credit, we in Owen Sound were grateful to be able to put forty people to work. And, to be completely fair, the Act itself was a credit to Mr. Robarts, his Ministers and his Government.

The interest was intense and the industry showed signs of getting on its feet. The firm was struggling and received constant supervision from Queen's Park until Election Day September 25. Then, on September 26th—the day after the election when the Conservative Candidate was defeated—the order came to close the plant down. This order came from Mr. Mitchell who is the assistant to Mr. Echin, the Director of ODA. The day after the election, some forty people in Owen Sound lost their jobs.

"While commending the government on its help to this point, I cannot condone as a member of this legislature the complete disregard for the rights of these people and their jobs. I cannot condone the spending of $150,000 in an obvious effort to secure the election of the Conservative candidate."[5]

CHAPTER 5

Bill's First Venture into Political Life

Bill went from his one room, eight grade pubic school to the only public high school in Owen Sound at that time. He was a student at the Owen Sound Collegiate Vocational Institute (OSCVI). At that time, the Robarts plan for education had just been implemented in the public school system of Ontario. When Bill arrived at OSCVI, the plan had been around long enough that the first floor of the school was where the four-year tech boys were situated. The third floor was the home of the four-year commercial girls, and the second floor was the home of the elite five-year academic scholars.

The wording used in the previous paragraph helps the reader see the attitude of the educational world to the Robarts plan. Most of the teachers in the secondary school had been educated under a system in which every student was an academic. Those who failed dropped out of school and joined the work force. Those who passed through the five years could go on to university, teachers college, or nursing.

The biggest problem with the new Robarts plan was that a number of the academic subject teachers (i.e. English, History, Math, Science, etc.) couldn't adjust their assessment and evaluation of the new four-year students to allow these students to receive marks in the 80s and 90s. For these teachers, there was no such thing as a marking system that was tailored to the new four-year stream. In this structure, the teacher could not give an 80 per cent to the four-year students at a different level of marking than that used for the academic students receiving 80 per cent. In a number of cases, teachers "looked down their noses" and didn't really want to teach academics to this new four-year stream.

Bill was entering OSCVI as a member of this four-year technical group. On top of this, Bill wasn't from Owen Sound. A number of students in the academic stream frowned upon students who were not from the city.

When Bill decided to run for head boy, he did so as a four-year tech student from outside of Owen Sound. In the relatively short history of the Robarts plan, no one had ever been elected head boy from either the four-year tech or the four year commercial programs even though the number of students in these new programs was sufficient to elect one of their own.

For years, the campaign for head boy and head girl had been a highlight of the school year. There was even a parade into downtown Owen Sound. That year, however, the principal made the decision that there was to be no campaigning, no parade, and next to no poster campaign. Bill went to the principal, stating that the campaign for student body leadership was always an exciting time for the school. This was Bill's first appeal, and he lost. The principal did not change his mind; however, Bill was successful in overcoming the obstacles that he faced and won the election.

This victory brought Bill into another conflict with the principal. There were three clubs with social standing in the school. The head boy had always been a member of the most elite club. Bill was not. The principal suggested that he should leave his club to join the more "politically correct" one. There was no question in Bill's mind—he would continue in the club of which he was already a member.

CHAPTER 6

The Tombstones

The 1960s saw the rise of the beginning of many changes in society. The emergence of rock and roll bands was one of these changes. The Rolling Stones and The Beatles were two of these groups. These were the most famous of the groups, but each secondary school and each community had their own groups, and it usually was more than one group. At OSCVI, The Tombstones was one of these groups.

Bill states that he had no training and very little background in music, but he volunteered to be the group's manager. The group had very few bookings, so Bill said that he would get them a booking in Walter's Falls. Bill soon had the group travelling around the province with bookings in Wasaga Beach and Sauble Beach. They even visited the well-known Hawk's Nest of the 1960s and '70s (Ronnie Hawkins' club in Toronto) for the purpose of working on their own style.

The group didn't have much money, and the age of the availability of sound equipment had not yet arrived. Harry Parker was one of Owen Sound's great musicians, and he also had sound equipment. On many occasions Bill went to Harry to beg for and borrow equipment. The group sometimes paid Harry, but on other occasions Harry did not charge them, nor did he care to remember that the group had some of his equipment. Harry Parker was interested in helping young musicians succeed. He himself would twice win the over sixty-five senior fiddle contest at the world famous Shelburne annual competition. It is interesting to note that Bill was the chairperson at the Hepworth induction to the area's Music Hall of Fame in 2015 when Mr. Parker was inducted.

The Tombstones carried a coffin in the old 1949 fluid driven hearse that they'd picked up at a local wrecking yard. This hearse carried the group to each of their venues. The coffin was at the front of the stage while the group performed.

One of the venues where the groups had an engagement was in Parry Sound. While the group was preparing for the dance, Bill went to an area wrecker's yard. He discovered a late 1950s Cadillac hearse. He could purchase it for $350, which is what the Tombstones were being paid for their evening's presentation. Bill bought it; needless to say, there was no cash left for the group for their night in Parry Sound.

The next adventure was to get the hearse back to Owen Sound. It was decided that they would chain the unlicensed vehicle to the old Dodge hearse and drive the newer Cadillac behind it. Everything was going well until the Dodge quit running in the Collingwood area.

A police officer came along and asked them what they were doing. After a brief conversation, the officer told them to just get going and get the vehicle out of the area.

The restored hearse made an appearance at an OSCVI reunion years after the group had disbanded. It brought back many happy memories to former students, and members of the group Bill, Arnie Clark, George Dahmer, Neil Glenn, Dave Fernal, Dennis Scott, Ted Draper, and Jim Wayner. All are original Tombstone members. For Bill, the adventures with the Tombstones were only the beginning of a lifetime of working with musical groups and producing functions for them to perform at.

CHAPTER 7

Post High School Days

Bill was typical of many young men of the '60s. He had very long hair and later added the beard that has been part of his profile ever since. The hair became shorter when he became a member of the workforce.

Bill was in no hurry to join the workforce. He was managing the Tombstones, and he was very comfortable living at home where his parents lovingly provided him with a great family environment. A year after graduation, Bill began using his technical education from high school at various local companies. His skill in drafting was very important in his new work world. Although he was often paid as a labourer, he worked in the office performing various tasks that required drafting skills.

During one of his jobs, he worked for a brief time with a young lady who was developing a map of the Owen Sound area. This young lady didn't realize that Bill enjoyed telling stories that sounded true but were almost completely fictional.

When Bill was looking at the map, he asked the young woman why she hadn't included Fort Loon. Bill stated that Fort Loon was situated just outside of Bognor on the river, and that native traders used to come to the Fort using the river as their mode of transportation. They would carry on their businesses with the local merchants at Fort Loon.

The young lady didn't realize that the twinkle in Bill's eye was a sign that he was telling a story. Fort Loon had existed as a play fort that Bill had in his play area in Bognor.

Bill later discovered that Fort Loon was added to the map. His story telling was never meant to be harmful, so the map had to be fixed. He was able to get the map, and using his drafting skills, remove Fort Loon. As his long time secretary, Sandra Breedon, learned, one needs to look for the twinkle in Bill's eyes to see if he's simply having fun with a story, or if it's really the truth.

Bill worked for CPI Paints and for A.P. Green Refractories, where he helped build furnaces to melt the glass. He spent four years with Edwards in a job that involved a lot of repetitive tasks.

He ventured out to Quebec at the time of the F.L.Q. crisis. Although he was in the heart of the area of the crisis, he didn't have any difficulties, because he mixed with the population of the area.

His mode of travel at this time was his motorcycle. He was one of the founders of the motorcycle group in the Owen Sound area called the Saddle Tramps, a connection that he has kept to this day. A new job found Bill working for Imperial Oil. This job took him to Halifax, where he was responsible for the payroll. There were three shifts as the Imperial Oil facility operated twenty-four hours a day. Bill was responsible for maintaining the payroll records for all three shifts. Although he put in long hours, he also was able to hire three assistants—one being responsible for each of the shifts. Bill was always anxious to get back to his beloved Bognor, so the adventure to Halifax was just that—an event that happened.

CHAPTER 8

A Motorcycle Man

Life for Bill has always been enjoyable. It can be said that his life, and the lives of those around him, have often been hectic, but fun.

Bill had an early love for motorcycles, so it's not surprising that one of his earliest purchases was a bike. It's typical of Bill that he never wants his enjoyment to be just for himself. It wasn't long until he was one of the leaders in the development of a bike club. This club would become known as Saddle Tramps Motorcycle Club.

The name "Saddle Tramp" originated in Texas in the early twentieth century as a term to describe itinerant workers who came to Texas to work on ranches. Most of these saddle tramps soon moved on to other places.

"Saddle Tramps" has become a much-used term. There was even a recording group called Saddle Tramps that reached the high point of its popularity in the 1960s. Many other biker clubs have used this name as their title. A number of them have continuous trouble with the law, especially because of their involvement with the drug trade. Others were not well liked because of their way of life, which led society to consider them as outlaws to society. The Owen Sound group never has been known for creating problems for society, yet because they were bikers there were those in the community who frowned upon them.

Bill hasn't been active as a biker for a long time. On the other hand, he's not a person to forget old friends. He's always been aware of the Saddle Tramps' activities as a group and has maintained contact with some of the original members.

Doug "Dudley" MacMillan was one of those original members. Doug is a Bognor boy. When he passed away in early October, 2015, his old buddy from Bognor was asked to participate in the eulogy. Many bikers from across the province came to pay tribute to Dudley, who was known for helping others without expecting anything in return. His daughter said that she was overwhelmed by the number of people at the wake who stated that their lives had been touched by her father. She went on to say that her father would be deeply missed by her and her children, because he was a great family man.

Doug had travelled with the bikers on their many charity runs. Like Bognor Bill, he never lost his love of the farm, and particularly horses. Dudley loved the Bognor area and all of its beauty. The Maverick did it again. The once "not acceptable" biker group called the Owen Sound Saddle Tramps has become a very respectable part of the community.

No group receives greater tribute for what it does than the Salvation Army. Doug "Dudley" McMillan's family suggested that one of the places to which memorial contributions could be directed was the Salvation Army.

By the way, when one sees a picture of Bognor Bill on a bike, make sure that the gleam in his eyes is observed. In his heart, Bognor Bill is still a biker.

CHAPTER 9

Interlude Two

On the Murdoch property in East Upper Bognor stands a building called the "Chicken Coop." It could be called Bill's office, his storehouse, or a place that keeps his wife happy, because most of Bill's piles and piles of memorabilia and other artifacts are found in this "museum."

One of the pictures hanging up in the Chicken Coop is a portrait of Agnes MacPhail. This picture is not hidden away, but is on the wall in a place where you cannot help but see it. Agnes "Aggie" MacPhail is certainly a Grey County maverick and a woman that Bill holds in high esteem.

It was 1919, the year after World War II ended. The war years had been a time when women were needed to work in industry and the war effort, because so many men were directly involved with the war. Canadian society came to realize that women should be given the right to vote. The right was given in 1919. Two years later, that Maverick country elected the very first woman to the Canadian parliament. There are those who would like to classify the area of Grey as "Red Neck" country. Grey certainly has its share of rednecks, but the fact that it elected Canada's first female MP helps to put the stamp on it as maverick country.

Agnes MacPhail was born in southwest Grey. She was born as Agnes McPhail and is buried in the McPhail family plot, but she changed the spelling of her name to MacPhail when she visited Scotland and discovered that her ancestors spelt the name that way.

She was born a farmer's daughter in a conservative family whose father believed that a woman's job was in the kitchen, and that a woman was meant to be of utmost importance in raising a family. Agnes was never interested in doing household work, nor was she ever interested in getting married.

Many of the men from the neighbourhood gathered in the McPhail living room on almost a weekly basis to discuss the problems of the world. Agnes listened to these discussions with open ears and developed a strong desire to help people.

In spite of her father's opposition to her getting an education, Agnes would read and study in secret. Her father loved her, and even though he was against it, Agnes went to school to become a teacher. After a few years of teaching, however, the itch to be in politics took hold of her life.

Many were the men of South Grey who were amazed that she won the nomination in 1921. They were even further amazed that she won the election. She became an avid member of the socialist Ginger Group faction of the Progressive Party, which was one of the leading contributors to the formation of the Cooperative Commonwealth Federation (CCF).

Agnes became the first president of the Ontario CCF in 1932, but she left it in 1934 when the United Farmers of Ontario broke from the organization because of the fear that it was becoming a communist group.

Agnes never forgot her farm roots. In fact, she even wrote agricultural articles for the *Toronto Globe and Mail*. On the other hand, even though she left the CCF group, she maintained close communication with many of its members.

Agnes was a pacifist, yet she voted in favour of Canada entering World War II.

During her years in the Canadian parliament, and later as a member of the Ontario legislature, Ms. MacPhail was always a spokesperson for the rural people of her riding. She also was responsible for the passing of a bill that led to major reforms in the penal systems. One of her last acts at Queen's Park was to ensure the passage of the first bill ever passed by the legislature seeking equal pay for women. It became official legislation in 1951.

CHAPTER 10

Bognor Forever

Following the wedding of Bill's younger brother, John, to Cathy, Bill and Sue began to date. Cathy and Sue had been best friends since their school days and had grown up in the same neighbourhood of Owen Sound. Bill had known Sue for a long time before the wedding, but he only became serious about this young lady, who was now a nurse, following his brother's wedding. For Bill, dating Sue meant that he had to get serious about a job and settling down.

After their wedding they lived with Bill's parents for the first year. They then purchased the land to the east of Bognor that was once owned by a good friend of Dick Murdoch, Bill Armstrong. This is a wonderful property from which one can look out to the west, north, and south from many points and see the total beauty of the area. East Upper Bognor, as Bill has named the area of the property, has been the Murdoch home for over forty-two years.

One cannot forget Bill and John's younger sister, Elizabeth, who was also a member of John and Cathy's wedding party. Not only was she John's little sister, but she'd also become a friend of Cathy's when they were attending West Hill Secondary School in Owen Sound.

Elizabeth married Gord Harris. They began Grey-Bruce Coating and Insulation, which is found on Side Road 6 at the edge of Bognor. You'll pass this business on the left as you travel to East Upper Bognor. If you should happen to go into the Grey-Bruce Coating building, one of the people that you are bound to see is Cathy Murdoch, who has been working for her brother-in-law and sister-in-law for almost forty years.

She currently serves as the company's bookkeeper, as well as tending to many other tasks for the company. Cathy and John live in Bognor. Bognor Bill was also an employee for a year in the early days of the company.

Dick and Betty's children have remained close to each other. The three families regularly went home to Dick and Betty's to spend Christmas morning together, even when their own families were growing up. Betty passed away in 2004. Another tradition that the three children continued throughout the years was to go home to Mother's for Sunday dinner. The three women—Sue, Cathy, and Elizabeth, are often companions on shopping trips.

Sue and Cathy have enjoyed their love of singing. They both have spent many years as members of the Sweet Adeline club in Owen Sound. Susan was one of the members of the club who went to a convention in Las Vegas in the early fall of 2015. She had just returned to Owen Sound on an important birthday date for her. The Sweet Adeline club had their regular gathering on the night of her birthday. Bill arrived as the practice was ending with a birthday cake for all to celebrate, but this was not the real celebration. The real celebration would take place that Friday night in Meaford when John and Cathy, Elizabeth and Gord, and Bill and Susan would have dinner together.

Since Bill and Susan moved to East Upper Bognor, many great events have happened in their lives. Nothing was greater or more important than the birth of their two daughters, Karen and Angie. The two girls spent their childhood and teenage years on this beautiful property before moving on to their fulfilling adult lives.

Ron Pegg

CHAPTER 11

East Upper Bognor

Bill and Sue needed a home to live in on their new property, which was named the "Murdoch Village Ranch." A trailer was purchased and moved to the ranch. To this day, that trailer is the centrepiece of their home. A short time later the first log building, which was built in Bognor in 1850 by James Potter, was moved log by log to the ranch. The log building had been a play area for Bill and his friends as they were growing up. These logs were used to enhance the trailer as the house was expanded. Other expansions have happened through the years, including an upstairs sun deck looking out over the Bognor area.

Over the years, the ranch has been the home of the Murdoch Cattle Company, which is a cow-calf operation. It also housed a fine stable of horses, and Bill often used his barns to shelter other people's horses. His pet donkey, Carl, roams the property as if it was his.

Thousands of cedar, pine, and spruce trees have been planted to beautify the property, but even more importantly as part of Bill's continuous interest in conservation, as the trees provide a habitat for wildlife.

Bill loves to spend time on this property working and enjoying necessary tasks such as haying and fencing. He has fed thousands of wild birds and has constructed many bluebird boxes. The birds are not particularly disturbed by the many cats that inhabit the ranch.

A second trailer was brought onto the property more recently. This became the Chicken Coop. It has a crafted chicken sitting on its deck, making it an agricultural building to house Bill's archives.

It's interesting to drive from Bognor up the road to this unique property. At the edge of Bognor stands a new bridge, which was necessary to build as the old bridge was no longer safe. However, the road up to East Upper Bognor is not paved, nor is it even updated. This is the road that leads to the home of a long time MPP who earlier in his career was on the local council and who even served as Warden of Grey County. It's a perfect example of how Bognor Bill is in reality a plain old country boy whose main interest in being in government has been to help other people.

It's interesting that another former Warden of Grey County, Murray Betts, has a similar situation. Murray was the undisputed Reeve of Artemesia for two decades. He was in County Council a decade before Bill's arrival. They are good friends. The road in Artemesia that goes by the Betts' home could probably use a good upgrade, but like the road that leads up to the Murdoch Village Ranch, it's a country gravel road. These are politicians whose main concern is the people they represent.

Wherever Bill is, there's bound to be music. The Bognor Jam was held on the ranch for a number of years. This was a weekend of rock and blues that was organized by Bill.

We visited with Bill in the fall of 2015 on days that he was not on the radio and had no other events that he needed to attend. Before we arrived at mid morning, Bill had already been out and about on the ranch. As we were leaving, he was heading back out to complete some chores.

Bognor Bill

CHAPTER 12

A New Career

When Bill's Uncle Walter decided to run for the position of deputy reeve in Sydenham Township, he encouraged his nephew to join him on his political journey and run for town council. Two years later, Bill led the polls in his next re-election bid.

After four years he was feeling constrained by being just a councillor, so he decided to challenge Sydenham's long serving reeve—something that is often considered a political "no- no." Bill not only won the election, but he got as many votes as the incumbent in the incumbent's home poll. Murdoch ran for re-election and was successful. He served for eight years in this capacity.

As the reeve he was also a member of County Council. Both in his position as a county councillor and as Reeve of Sydenham, one of his big concerns was the Niagara Escarpment Commission. It was too powerful. Because the escarpment runs through Sydenham, Bill was very aware of this.

His main concern centred on the very strict rules that the Commission insisted on enforcing. The Commission did not want to see any building activity on the escarpment. As much of the land was owned by the province, Bill had no problem with this public land being highly regulated. His concern was for the small landowners who had owned their property for many years. It was next to impossible—if not entirely impossible—for these people to make any changes or even build an addition to their homes. For many of these property holders, the property was the major source of their investments, and they couldn't make changes. It was nearly impossible to sell the properties, because potential buyers were aware of the severe restrictions. The Niagara Escarpment Commission showed no mercy.

In his various capacities, Bill continuously tried to help these small owners, but he had little success. In his mind, it was extremely unfair to these people who were voters in Sydenham and the surrounding areas, and they had no way of escaping this situation.

In 1987, Bill was elected Warden of Grey County by his peers. These same peers always enjoyed Bognor Bill and his outgoing personality. Ken MacIntyre from the Priceville area is one of these people. Ken has a beard that is very similar to Bill's.

On one occasion when they were both attending a function at the Holland-Chatsworth school, Bill, with the twinkle in his eye, said that he and Ken should stand side by side as the people left the auditorium. Ken was not as well known in that area as Bill. As the people came out, some shook hands with Bill while others shook hands with Ken. The people were really not sure which one was Bognor Bill.

The same two men were in an egg race at a summer event in Durham. The egg was carried on a spoon, and Ken easily won the race. Bill accused him of having the egg glued to the spoon, so Ken responded that the real truth was that Bognor Bill was just too slow. Bob McKessock was the Liberal MPP for the Durham area at that time. He and Bill played ball in the same league around Bognor. Mr. McKessock came over after the race and congratulated Bill on winning the race. He honestly didn't realize that it was the other man with the beard who had won.

Murdoch served on the Association of Municipalities of Ontario for five years and was the vice chair for two years. Probably his greatest interest was conservation, which is why it's somewhat ironic that he was continuously upset by the Niagara Escarpment Commission. As part of his interest in conservation, he spent five years as the Chair of the Grey Sauble Conservation Committee.

The word irony can often be used to describe Bognor Bill. When the encyclopedia researchers were compiling information on Bill, they concluded that it's very difficult to describe Bill Murdoch's political philosophy. The person writing the article didn't understand or appreciate that it's very easy to describe his philosophy. It goes something like this—if it's good for his constituents, then it's good. If it's not good for his constituents, then it's not good. And add to this that this Grey County Maverick has always been his own person.

Bill would be the first to admit that he's not perfect, although his wife might think it (not say it) before Bill would say it. Bob Elliott, the former Reeve of Flesherton, tells the story of being on a local conservation bus trip that included the Bognor area. While they were travelling through the Murdoch Ranch, one of the people noticed that what was happening in front of their eyes was contrary to what Bill was promoting. Bill quickly responded: "Do as I say, not as I do." An honest maverick response!

CHAPTER 13

"Queen's Park—Here He Comes!"

It was 1987. It would be the only election that he would ever lose. David Peterson and his Liberal Party were swept into office in a landslide victory. In the riding of Grey, Ron Lipsett, a new Liberal candidate, defeated the future Grey County maverick by two thousand votes. However, by the year 1990, the glow had quickly faded from the Peterson government. They still controlled the government, but in the Grey riding Bill Murdoch was the winner with Peggy Hutchinson, the NDP candidate, coming in second—two thousand five hundred votes behind Bill. Ron Lipsett dropped to third place.

The Maverick became only the fifth representative for the southern part of Grey in almost seventy years. Farquhar Oliver had been its representative for over forty years. The only two representatives that the area elected and later defeated during this time were Eric Winkler, who was defeated by Bob McKessock in 1975 by two hundred votes, and Murdoch, who defeated Lipsett in 1990. When Murdoch retired, he was the second longest serving member after Oliver.

The Peterson Liberals stayed in power for the next five years. During those years, Murdoch served in many different roles. Drawing upon his background in municipal affairs, he served as the opposition critic on Municipal Affairs for his first three years. He also spent a year as the Management Board and Cabinet critic. He then became the critic for Agriculture, Northern Development, and Transportation for a year. He was also on a number of various standing committees during this first term, including the Ombudsman and General Government committees.

In the election of 1995, Bill became part of the Mike Harris Conservative government in Ontario. He had now been in Queen's Park for five years. Because of his work as a critic, he wasn't an unknown. He'd also presented a number of petitions and bills. The bills were a strong indication that the representative from Grey was very concerned for his constituents. In 1993, he introduced an Act to help the Owen Sound Little Theatre get on its feet. In the same year he introduced legislation to help local municipalities. Another piece of legislation he introduced concerned tax exemptions. In 1994, he presented a petition on the subject of the Human Rights Code.

His love of conservation and his desire to help the small land owners in the province drove Bill to introduce legislation in both 1991 and 1992 to try to change the Acts dealing with the Niagara Escarpment and the surrounding wet lands. Laws like these that governed the escarpment to the detriment of his constituents were at the very heart of the Maverick's desire to be in the legislature. Changes were needed.

CHAPTER 14

Tartan Day

The number of people in North America who can include Scotland as part of their heritage far outnumber the Scots who live in Scotland. In the area of Grey, there are a number of locales in which the first white settlers were from Scotland. The Scots are very proud of their heritage, but these same Scots are proud Canadians. They have worked the land and have been outstanding Canadian citizens, evidenced by their involvement in war and in roles of leadership in government. John A MacDonald, Canada's first prime minister, was Scottish.

In the early 1980s, Mrs. Jean Watson, a resident of Nova Scotia, began promoting the idea of setting aside a day on the Canadian calendar on which to honour the Scots. Mrs. Watson relentlessly worked at soliciting support amongst politicians and Scottish groups. Eventually, Nova Scotia adopted "Tartan Day."

Mrs. Watson was not satisfied with just Nova Scotia. She began to reach out across Canada. One of the people who heard about her efforts was the recently elected member from Grey. Very few people are as proud of their Scottish heritage as Bill Murdoch.

The new legislative member proposed a private members bill that passed on December 19, 1991, making April 6 Tartan Day. In many other areas where there are special recognition days for the Scots, the day of celebration is held on July 1. As that date is Canada Day; it would not have been an appropriate day; therefore, April the 6 was chosen. By the year 2000, every province and territory in Canada, with the exception of Quebec, had adopted Tartan Day.

In the Ontario legislature, the bill passed with complete support from all three parties. One person who spoke at length in support of the bill was the MPP from Scarborough, a member of the Liberal caucus, Alvin Curling. Curling was born in Jamaica. He is the first member of the Legislature to come from this island.

Curling once staged a sit-in at the Legislature over one of the bills presented by the Mike Harris government, due to the lack of public consultation. Like Bill, Curling represents his constituents with passion. In spite of the many changes in government from Liberal to NDP, Conservative, and then back to Liberal, Curling maintained his seat. When the Liberals came back into power under Dalton McGuinty, he was selected as the Speaker of the House. He later resigned to become Canada's envoy to the Dominican Republic.

Curling adopted the title for himself "man of the people."

Murdoch

CHAPTER 15

The Black Bear Hunt

Following the election of the Harris government in 1995, Bill was appointed the parliamentary assistant to the Minister of Northern Development and Mines. He would continue in this capacity until early June 1999.

In early 1999, the Natural Resources ministry under John Snobelen passed a bill that eliminated the Northern Ontario spring bear hunt. The ministry had been receiving pressure from environmentalists that the spring hunt was bad because it took place when baby bears were born, and in spite of pressures from the authorities to not shoot female bears, many were being killed. It's interesting that most of the environmental pressure came from Southern Ontario, where the population of black bears was very sparse compared to Northern Ontario where there was no scarcity.

There were already gun regulations in place to control the killing of bears. The great majority of bear hunting had to take place, as it does today, as a guided hunt. The country of the northern black bears is mainly an uninhabited human territory. It is a wilderness.

The Northern Ontario people felt strongly that the environmentalists from the south of the province, with a government minister from the urban area of Ontario, didn't understand. Mr. Snobelen had been moved to this Natural Resource portfolio from the Education portfolio because of the pressure that Snobelen was under. A number of educators felt that this high school dropout didn't have an understanding of the Education portfolio.

Of course, the Maverick felt that in his role as parliamentary assistant in the Department of Northern Development, he should make his understanding of the situation known, so he spoke against the bill. When it passed, he made a plea for more open votes in the Legislature. It was not long after this, that the Maverick was removed from his position as a parliamentary assistant. It's ironic that almost three years later he was appointed to the position of parliamentary assistant to the Minister of the Environment.

In the spring of 2016, the present Ontario Liberal government is bringing back the spring hunt. A major reason is public safety.

It's estimated that between fifty thousand and one hundred thousand black bears live in Northern Ontario, with the average weight of a bear being one hundred and seventy five pounds.

CHAPTER 16

Interlude 3

Most people probably wouldn't consider Farquhar Oliver as a maverick, so let's briefly look at this gentleman.

Born in Priceville at the turn of the century, he was elected as a United Farmers of Ontario candidate (U.F.O) in South Grey in 1926 at twenty-two years of age.

The U.F.O., which had formed the Ontario government under Ernest Drury, was already falling into disarray. The base of this political movement was farmers. When the leadership under Drury tried to broaden the base by including labourers, many of the farmers withdrew their support.

Under Drury, the Ontario Legislature established its first Department of Welfare. This department implemented Ontario's first allowances for women and children.

In the early 1930s, there was an attempt to have this movement join with the C.C.F., but the U.F.O. didn't want anything to do with this group because of their concerns that the C.C.F. had communist leanings. This was the final blow. The political movement that began in 1914 officially ended in 1934.

In the meantime, Mr. Oliver had continued winning his riding as a U.F.O. candidate. By 1934, he was the only member of the U.F.O. in the Legislature. He continued as a U.F.O. member with the blessing of the departed party until the early 1940s, when he officially joined the Liberals, whom he had supported since 1934.

The people of Grey were showing their maverick personality. When their member is the only one of a particular party in the Legislature for over a decade, it would appear that the people of the riding certainly were very supportive of this quiet, but highly respected, gentleman.

When Oliver officially joined the Liberals, he was immediately named to the Cabinet. However, when the leader of the party, Premier Mitch Hepburn, resigned as leader and appointed a new leader without consulting even his caucus, Mr. Oliver resigned from the Cabinet.

Once this problem was fully resolved with a new leader, Harry Nixon, in place, Oliver returned to the Cabinet as Deputy Leader. He had previously worked with Nixon in the Farmer's movement.

During the next two decades, Farquhar Oliver would serve as interim Liberal Party leader and the elected Liberal leader for almost ten years. The party was in disarray following the years of the Mitch Hepburn governments and was often the third party in its membership in the Legislature. The Conservatives controlled the legislature, with the C.C.F. usually being the official opposition. In the provincial election that Oliver fought as leader, the Liberals ended up in their usual third place. During these years, the Liberal Party's only stability was the maverick from Priceville who began as a U.F.O. member and ended up providing leadership for a dysfunctional Liberal Party.

CHAPTER 17

Walkerton

One of the first things that Mike Harris did after he was elected Premier was to have a long conversation with Bill Murdoch. Harris shared that he had a great deal of respect for the representative of Grey-Bruce Owen Sound. He also understood that Bill was a man whose principles were more important than his party allegiance. As a result, Bill would disagree with the party if the matter to be resolved was one in which Bill's desire to serve his constituents was different than the party's position. Harris told Bill that this was acceptable in the Legislature, but not at the Cabinet level. There must be unity in the Cabinet's position.

Because Mike Harris knew that Bill couldn't guarantee his complete unity with the Cabinet, he couldn't appoint Bill to any Cabinet position. Murdoch understood the Premier's position. No better example can be found of the correctness of this position than the Walkerton water crisis.

Walkerton is located in Bill's riding. In May 2000, an outbreak of E-coli resulted from contamination of the water system. This contamination was caused by the runoff from the many farm operations in the area where the fertilizer got into a Walkerton well. There had been concerns of this happening for some time, but the people in charge of the water had ignored what was happening. Even though there were tests that showed they should be concerned, they did nothing. The crisis in 2000 led to seven deaths and at least two thousand people becoming sick. There are still a number of people in 2016 that suffer from the effects of this contamination.

The Mike Harris government was hedging on what action should be taken. The Liberal opposition put together a bill for a committee to be formed to investigate the Walkerton crisis.

There was no question the Maverick would vote to support this legislation. These people were folks that he represented—there was no choice. Mr. Harris was fully aware of the Maverick's position. The Liberal proposal was reaching the stage where a vote was to be taken.

At this time, one of Mike Harris's staff members arrived at Bill's desk with the message that if the Maverick would not vote in favour of this proposition, the Conservatives would bring in their own proposition to establish an investigation. Murdoch voted against the Liberal motion.

The Conservative government's proposition passed, and an investigation took place. In 2004, two employees of Walkerton were found guilty of neglect and received sentences from the court. A complete new set of rules and regulations were introduced for the handling of water in Ontario.

Mr. Murdoch had successfully served his constituents and played a role in bringing in provincial rules that would protect the entire province. Mr. Harris had preserved party solidarity while at the same time allowing the Maverick to be a significant force in handling a major problem in the heart of his own riding that impacted the province as a whole.

CHAPTER 18

The First Speech

The Maverick's first speech to the Legislature defined who Bill was and who he was going to be. He never wavered. This speech was given on November 17, 1990.

> I am delighted to be able to address this House today by replying to the speech from the throne. I would like to thank the people of Grey and Owen Sound who elected me to represent them and who have given me the privilege of participating in this debate.
>
> I represent the riding of Grey. I follow in the footsteps of Eddie Sargent, who represented us in the Legislature for many years and who served his constituency well. I hope to be able to serve the people in Grey in the same caring manner.
>
> Grey is a diverse riding, with Owen Sound as its largest urban centre. We also have the towns of Hanover, Durham, Meaford, and Thornbury. There is a small manufacturing sector in the riding, but we would like to increase our tax base with the influx of clean industry.
>
> Most of our riding's revenue, however, comes from tourism and agriculture, both of which were ignored in last week's speech from the throne. I know that the NDP power base in the past had not come from either of these two communities, but I say to the Premier and his Cabinet that they cannot be overlooked. These two industries are vital to the wellbeing of

much of the province, not just of my riding, and their needs must be addressed.

In Grey, our agriculture community consists mainly of dairy, beef, pork, and sheep farmers. We also have a healthy apple industry, which produces some of the finest in Ontario.

Out tourist attractions are second to none. We have a four-season tourist area that attracts visitors all year to enjoy great skiing, beautiful walking trails, clean water and beaches and good fishing. I urge all members to see for themselves the fine recreational features my riding offers.

One of the loveliest areas in the province is the land in the Niagara Escarpment, and I feel very strongly that we should preserve its beauty for future generations. Its awesome beauty is there for all to admire, and I trust nothing will change that.

There is, however, land in my riding which is marginal at best and my goal is to achieve a sensitive balance between conservation and development in these areas. This is difficult at present because my constituents cannot fully realize all the land has to offer, because of the lack of democracy shown by the Niagara Escarpment Commission. In my view, the Commission has taken the decision-making away from the people who own the land, and this is not right. The land is theirs and they should have a say in its future.

Because the previous government offered few new initiatives to agriculture in the last five years, farmers have been forced to sell off parcels of land to survive. Unfortunately, this government does not appear as yet to rectify the situation. Some say that Grey leads the province in severances, but I challenge these figures. Even if they are true, however, I do not feel it is important, because we do have the needed land for sustainable and affordable development.

The contour of the land and tree cover is such that many building lots could be created and never noticed. It would not change the natural environment at all and would provide prime locations for people who wish to live there.

The issue of local autonomy comes up again in the government's treatment of municipalities across the province. I have been a long-time observer of the relations between the two levels of government and an active participant in the process. As a past member of the executive of AMO, as a local reeve and county warden, and as my party's critic for Municipal Affairs, I would urge this government not to intrude further into the lives of its people.

Because of my experience, I understand the importance of our municipal governments in the effective functioning of our province. They want and deserve a co-operative and consultative relationship with the province, rather than a dependent controlling one, in order that they may be responsive to the people who elect them. This level of government is closer to the people and more respectful of them than any other.

I feel it is incumbent on this government to listen to what people have to say rather than to lobby groups that often do not even live in the community but think they know what is best for the people who do.

In the last five years, we in Ontario have lost the partnership that had been built between Queen's Park and our municipalities. I urge this government to ensure not only that the relationship does not deteriorate further, but also to consult with local governments to determine what can be done to correct some of the problems.

I am hopeful that the $700 million mentioned in the throne speech will be divided fairly across the province to assist in achieving that goal. So much needs to be done. The population of the province outside Toronto is growing quickly and smaller centres do not have, and cannot afford, the infrastructure to support this growth.

If the province is going to be able to take the view that these centres must expand, then money is desperately needed. Water and sewer facilities must be expanded and highways must be upgraded. The roads in my riding are fast becoming very dangerous and I can only hope that this government will address the problem.

No mention was made of how or where this money will be spent. I hope, if it has not all been allocated as yet, that the Minister and the Treasurer will try to understand the present plight of these small communities.

As members know, the previous government excelled in announcing initiatives, which sounded wonderful, but upon examination came up with no funding to put them in place. This left the people of the province with high expectations and then greater disappointment when their local governments could not afford to deliver without huge municipal tax increases. This also was not fair and I hope this new government will not continue to place these burdens on our local councils.

Some of the smaller urban centres in the province now have very fragile economies and cannot afford to lose what industry they have. I was disappointed to note that there was nothing in the throne speech to address this issue and I hope the government will give its attention to this matter as quickly as possible.

I am afraid that measures such as the proposed environment bill of rights will indeed have the reverse effect and serve to drive industry away. I hope this is not the case, but I will examine the legislation closely and with the interests of smaller businesses in mind.

In closing, let me say once again how honoured I am to represent the voters of Grey and Owen Sound. I pledge to represent them to the best of my ability. I will be watching this government to ensure that my people's interests are addressed and I will work with them in order to meet Grey's and Owen Sound's goals and aspirations.

CHAPTER 19

"A Man for His Riding"

Bognor Bill was raised a small town boy in a home where his parents loved him and always cared for him. It is this small town boy and his family's belief in community that Bill took with him when he was elected to the Legislature.

The people of his riding always were very important to him. If the Maverick could help out in any way, he would. When a group of students from one of the schools in the riding visited the Legislature, he made sure that pictures with thanks were sent to the school for these students. He attended birthday party and anniversary celebrations throughout the riding. If there was a charity golf tournament, he was sure to be involved. When the Flesherton arena was gutted by a major fire, Murdoch attended the Chris Neil golf tournament, which was a major fundraiser for the reconstruction of this facility. The golf tournament concluded with a beef barbeque during which the awards for the day were presented. Bill had volunteered to cut the meat for an hour. He ended up cutting the meat for two and a half hours. This was not unusual. He loves to volunteer and help at these types of events.

Just a side note—the Maverick thought that it would be great to get a picture with Chris Neil of both of them with the plates for their front teeth out of their mouths. Many are the times that pictures of Neil have appeared with his teeth out. The Maverick's idea was that the words that would accompany the photographs would be: "We both fight for our team."

Murdoch was always a great supporter of Crime Stoppers, Big Brothers, Big Sisters, Girl Guides and Boy Scouts, the Canadian National

Institute for the Blind, Sydenham Sportsmen, the Owen Sound Salmon Spectacular, the Mount Forest and Hanover Scottish Bands … and the list goes on and on.

Bill has been classified as a friend of the people. He was willing to work side by side in riding matters when Ovid Jackson was the Liberal MP for the area. Ovid and Bill often made presentations together for the benefit of their people.

The election of 2003 saw the Conservative government under the leadership of its recently elected leader, Ernie Eves, soundly defeated by the Liberals. The Tory seats dropped from a majority of fifty-nine to twenty-four. The Maverick was one of the very successful twenty-four. Bill Murdoch's legislative aide from his legislature office in Toronto, Ana Sajfert, wrote the following about this time:

> I knew I wanted a front-row seat on his re-election campaign in 2003. The man was a local legend, and my journalistic curiosity naturally drove me to question how much of it was myth. To the outsiders, the riding of Bruce-Grey-Owen Sound was at times insignificant, but the Bognor native who represented it was not.
>
> Long before he hired me, a twenty-four-year-old reporter plying novice talents at the *Hanover Post*, Bill Murdoch had established his name in provincial politics. His half-crass, half-blunt but always genuine comments had occasionally graced the daily newspapers in Ontario since his election to provincial parliament in 1990. Reporters licked their chops when MPP Murdoch shamed his fellow Conservative ministers, or when he publicly challenged the party's leader, or when he accused the government of "stealing money" from Northern Ontario and warned the folk there to watch their backs as the government had it in for them. When MPP Murdoch spoke, the urban elites cringed, the rural folk listened, and the media clinched slam-dunk headlines.
>
> The only time I've seen MPP Murdoch pause reflectively was when he talked about the hardship, the work ethic, and the pride of his people at home. And that's what he liked to

call them: my people. I never doubted he had his people's back. That was one part of his genius. He had Bruce and Grey born and bred in his bones and always had the pulse of his people's needs and wants. The other part of his genius was that he truly listened to the people, albeit he didn't always agree with them.

The 2003 election felt bottled up with angst. Just three years earlier, the town of Walkerton was struck by tragedy after a spring storm contaminated the town's water supply, killing seven and leaving hundreds of people sick from E. coli. The local MPP said he fought on all fronts to get the public inquiry set up so the people of Walkerton can have their voices heard. While I was not on staff during these years and cannot speak to any details, I d know that the MPP was still putting out fires years after the fact, one of which later culminated in MPP Murdoch dropping the F-bomb on CBC Radio while firing back at the reporter.

So as expected, the writ period was hostile at times. Especially in the all-candidates' debate, a forum that MPP Murdoch always loathed. It was the Walkerton debate held at the Victoria Hall that made me appreciate his distrust and dislike of this forum. The hall was stacked with the opposing parties' supporters, and they were relentlessly shaming Murdoch. But he kept his cool. He had to. He knew he had to stick it out, fighting politics with good, not bad, emotions. So he stuck to his personal beliefs, which were that the people of Walkerton wanted to get on with rebuilding their lives.[6]

Ron Pegg

Bill with Larry Miller

80th birthday, June 13, 1996, at Harrision Park with Etta Allen and Ovid Jackson

Parade in Grey County

50

Bognor Bill

Assisting Bartender in Cuba

CHAPTER 20

In Opposition

Ernie Eves appears to have made the often-fatal mistake of running a very negative campaign. This campaign didn't help the already existing condition of dissatisfaction with the Harris government in which Eves had served as Treasurer. There were also the issues of a major hydro blackout, the SARS scare, and the Mad Cow problem.

The election also decimated the NDP. With an earlier change that lowered the number of seats in the Legislature, the Harris government in turn lowered the number of seats from twelve to eight for a political party to be considered a party and have all the rights that this status gives at Queen's Park. The NDP elected seven. They were one short.

The Maverick did not agree with the philosophy of the NDP—far from it. However, it's typical of Bill that although he disagrees with a person's ideas, he doesn't wish for this to destroy a personal relationship with the individual. He and Peter Kormos, an NDP maverick, had such a relationship. The two began to discuss the possibility of Murdoch joining the NDP caucus so that the NDP would have official party status. Bill was open to this discussion, because he felt that the people who had elected the seven deserved to have their voice heard. If he were to join the NDP, this would give the party full status. Nothing in Bill Murdoch's career better illustrates his desire to serve the people than this consideration to join the NDP. He would be doing this to help everyday people. In the meantime, however, a by-election took place, and an NDP member was elected. In reality, Bill was relieved.

The 2003 loss by the Eves government was the beginning for Murdoch of eight years as a member of the opposition. Murdoch liked to refer to this as "opposition wilderness." In the words of his secretary, Ana: "If wilderness meant survival, then survival we did . . ."

Part of this survival fight was with the Owen Sound daily paper, *The Sun Times*. In the words of Ana:

> Back at home, Murdoch kept up his fight with local media. He wasn't one to mince words, so when the Owen Sound *Sun Times* took a run at him for one thing or another, he pounced back. His most pronounced parry was to publicly denounce "the rag" and to block their reporters from our distribution list for media releases.
>
> Murdoch listened and heard people advise him against such ultimatums, but in the end as with other decisions, he did it his way.[7]

Fred Wallace has been on staff at the local radio station, CFOS, for over three decades. During these years, he has often been in the company of Bill. Fred, like Bill, has always been a great supporter of local events and fundraising activities. Both Bill and Fred have played roles in the local amateur theatre productions staged at the Roxy Theatre. They have been known to be at an event where both have had a turn at the microphone. Part of each of their comments would include a jest at each other. When Bill celebrated fifteen years in the legislature in 2005, the well-attended gala evening had as its Master of Ceremonies Fred Wallace.

Since Bill retired from politics, he has worked as the host of a morning phone in talk show at CFOS where Fred continues to work. Fred's major comment about the Maverick is that Murdoch is always passionate about what he believes. He wants to make those passions reality.

Fred remembers well the election night when Bill was speaking at the radio station to various news sources, and the local paper's reporter were barred from the event. Fred recalls one of the reporters being outside one of the windows trying to take a picture of events inside.

Why would Bill do this? It's relatively simple. Bill had always worked hard and passionately for the people of the riding. He believed that the local paper should have recognized this and supported his efforts. The failure of the paper to give this support was enough of a reason to bar them from the celebration events.

Tony Ambrosio worked alongside of Fred at CFOS in the 1980s and 1990s. He came to know Bill. Each man had a mutual respect for the other. When an opening came in the Toronto office in 1999, Tony was ready for a career change. For the next three years he went to work for Bill.

In Tony's words:

> There has probably been no one at Queen's Park who has worked harder for the people in his/her constituency than Bill Murdoch. Mr. Murdoch's concern in helping his constituents and working for them as individuals was done at the cost of any Cabinet post, and even led to him not being a parliamentary assistant to any Cabinet Minister for more than a short time. His belief in his people and their rights was always the consuming passion in this man from Grey.

A couple of practical examples that Mr. Ambrosio recalls are Bill getting the lights on Highway 10 at Dundalk and getting some special grants for the local hospital.

CHAPTER 21

Interlude 4

Winston Churchill did not come from Grey County. He probably never even heard of Grey County, but the great war leader of World War II from England, whose mother was American, would have fit in well with the maverick spirit of Grey.

Dwight D. Eisenhower worked side by side with Mr. Churchill in World War II and was later President of the United States in the 1950s for eight years. He wrote about Churchill in the book *Never Give In*.

On the eve of the Nazi invasion of Poland in September, 1939, Winston Churchill—his sixty-fifth birthday a little more than three months off—could look back on a long lifetime distinguished by more success in more careers than could most men of his age.

He had been a combat soldier on the Empire's far frontiers; a political leader not bound to partisan machine, for he had changed party affiliations when conviction so dictated; a principal architect of Britain's naval greatness in World War I; a strategist of that war whose daring plan, if it had been daringly executed, might have saved many millions of lives; a newspaper correspondent and author whose works in history and in biography had won him enduring fame.

In that season of 1939, his present was controversial and his future obscure: he was the prophet unheeded. Through the years, sometimes almost alone, his voice had been raised in warnings against Nazi aggression, in pleas that Britain prepare for war. His warnings were soon fully to be realized, although his pleas had been inadequately answered.

But the man, at once so restlessly impatient at getting things done personally and so eager for information at first-hand, could not abide by any fixed schedule. Often, unheralded, he descended on me to present a new idea, to argue once again a rejected proposal, to get the latest word on battle—or just to chat.[8]

This same book refers to a number of Mr. Churchill's greatest inspirational and well known speeches.

Come then. Let us to the task, to the battle, to the toil—each to our part, each to our station. Fill the armies, rule the air, pour out the munitions, strangle the U-boats, sweep the mines, plough the land, build the ships, guard the streets, succor the wounded, uplift the downcast, and honour the brave. Let us go forward together in all parts of the Empire, in all parts of the island. There is not a week, nor a day, nor an hour to lose. — Manchester, January 27, 1940

I would say to the House, as I said to those who have joined this Government: "I have nothing to offer but blood, toil, tears, and sweat." We have before us many, many long months of struggle and suffering. You ask: "What is our policy?"

I will say: "It is to wage war by sea, land, and air with all our might, and with all the strength that God can give us; to wage war against a monstrous tyranny, never surpassed in the dark lamentable catalogue of human crime." That is our policy. You ask: "What is our aim?"

I can answer in one word: "Victory!" Victory at all costs, victory in spite of all terror, victory however long and hard the road may be; for without victory there is no survival. —House of Commons, May 13, 1940

I am a child of the House of Commons; I was brought up in my father's house to believe in democracy. "Trust the people," was his message . . . In my country, as in yours, public men are proud to be servants of the State and would be ashamed to be its masters. —United States Congress, December 1941

CHAPTER 22

"And the Wilderness Continues"

The wilderness began with Ernie Eves as the leader of the Conservatives. He would soon retire. Mr. Eves had been an MPP for twenty years when he resigned for personal reasons. He had held the very difficult portfolio of Finance in the Harris government. When he campaigned for the party leadership, he faced the man who had replaced him in the finance portfolio—Jim Flaherty.

After the Eves government was defeated, another leadership convention took place. The two major candidates were John Tory and Jim Flaherty. John Tory portrayed himself as a moderate, and in the second round of ballots he defeated Jim Flaherty, who was from the right of the party. The vote gave Tory five hundred forty nine of the votes compared to Flaherty's four hundred sixty nine.

It's interesting that the Maverick's wilderness would intensify under John Tory. It's also very interesting that Jim Flaherty would soon resign from provincial politics and run federally. He eventually became the "man of the hour" in the Harper government and in Canada for so successfully leading the nation through the 2008 financial downturn in the market world.

In 2005, the Maverick celebrated fifteen years as a member in the Legislature from Grey.

It was time for a celebration, and there was a gala tribute. The event was organized by the Bruce-Grey Owen Sound provincial Progressive Conservative Association and the staff at the Queen's Park and Owen Sound Constituency office. Entertainment was provided by Willie O'

Hagan, known as the Irish Troubadour, and the renowned comedian, Country Clem. The relatively new Conservative Party leader, John Tory, was the special guest, and Fred Wallace was the Master of Ceremonies. A number of Murdoch's fellow MPPs were in attendance, as well as Larry Miller, who was now the area's Conservative MP in Ottawa.

A special tribute was spoken by one of Bill's long time associates in the Legislature, Chris Stockwell:

Good evening, ladies and gentlemen.

I'm glad to be here tonight, and honoured to have a chance to speak. To help you thank and pay tribute to Bill and Sue, thank them both for all they've done, and all that they've meant to the people of this part of Ontario.

I think it was Ralph Waldo Emerson who wrote that in order to make a friend, you have to first be a friend. Being a good friend is second nature to Bill Murdoch, and that's one of the reasons why so many of us are here tonight. And I've felt very lucky indeed to be the recipient of his friendship in the fifteen years we've served together at Queen's Park.

In Ontario politics today, Bill Murdoch is a living legend, an original, a renegade when necessary, but above all, he's loyal to the people who sent him to Queen's Park to represent their values and interests. All of you here.

Tonight's been a lot of fun, and we've laughed together about the past, and been reminded of some of the things Bill's done and accomplished. But I want to leave you all tonight thinking about the future—a future that includes keeping Bill Murdoch in the Legislature for a long time yet to come. Making sure that the voice of Grey and Bruce Counties and Owen Sound continues to be heard; that the challenges facing rural Ontario are not overlooked; that the "powers that be," or the "centre" as we called it, or the "pimply-faced Nazis" as Bill sometimes refers to them, whoever's in government, that they aren't able to take away the right of an MPP to represent his or her people; and that the blunt, unvarnished truth continues to be told.

So I close, thanking you, Bill and Sue, for this great night, for the past fifteen years, and for the future, where your greatest contribution to the people of Ontario is yet to come.

CHAPTER 23

Reflecting Back

The Maverick was always the Maverick. He has often spoken out on issues that others might mumble about but would not speak about. This was true when the Conservatives formed the government as well as when they were in the wilderness.

Murdoch's speech in the House on April 4, 1996, is evidence of his boldness:

> It certainly gives me pleasure to speak to this motion today, and to Mr. Brown from Algoma-Manitoulin. Some of his resolution is good and some of it is not so good. I thought we should talk about it and go through it.
>
> His resolution says, "That in the opinion of this House, since the northern Ontario heritage fund belongs to northern Ontario…" There's nothing wrong with that and I certainly agree with that. That's a good statement and I think we all can agree with that, that the fund does belong to northern Ontario and that's where it will stay. There's no problem with that statement in your resolution.
>
> It says the fund "represents a small share of the resource revenues to the province from the resource sector." Right on. I can agree with you on that—no problem with that. That is right on and there's no problem with that. The resources in the north should be shared by the north. For too long have the resources

gone to southern Ontario and the north hasn't had its share. I will agree with you on that—no problem there.

The fund "is an important tool for improving economic, social, and health conditions in the north." Right; that's what it was for. Unfortunately, sometimes with some of the previous governments it was given to different people who made unfair trading, unfair commerce, things like that. But you're right, that's what it was supposed to be used for, and we can agree with that, can agree with that all the way.

Now we get into some trouble. "And since the former New Democratic Party government transferred the legacy of northerners to the consolidated revenue fund of the province of Ontario…" That's a shameful thing. We just heard from one of the ministers of the previous government that had six or seven ministers from the north and did absolutely nothing for the north—stole money from the north, stole the money and put it in the revenue fund so that when they had an election they wouldn't look as bad as they were. They left us with a $100-billion debt and they stole $60 million from the northern fund to try to cover it up. They stole it right out of the fund, put it into the revenue, thinking all the time—and I don't know how they ever felt this—that they would win the election and they'd be able to sneak it back in and nobody would know.

Then we have the former Treasurer stand up and say this is a lie. I'm disappointed that he would do that. I know he did a lot of things in the past five years: put us $50 billion more in debt, left us with a $100-billion debt, $10 billion a year in debt he put this province in, and then stole $60 million out of the north, which he represents, along with six or seven other ministers. They were in the north and did absolutely nothing for the north and then they can stand here today and talk about how they looked after the north?

This is utterly ridiculous, utterly ridiculous. Here's what they did: They took away the money from the north, from their own legacy, stole the money.

He goes on to say, "Premier Harris has expressed his deep concern about the disappearance of the funds from the trust account. This is true."

And then there was Bill's great speech about the telephone. The Maverick made this speech on February 13, 1997:

It is with great pleasure that I rise today to speak on this resolution. As you know, the 20th century is about to come to a close. The 20th century will be remembered for many of its advancements in technology that have made life easier and more enjoyable for all of us: inventions like the vehicle, the television, the computer, and the telephone, just to name a few. But before we move ahead into the 21st century, I think it's necessary to take another look at the telephone.

Since its introduction, business people, politicians, friends and family have enjoyed the ability to talk to each other at the touch of a dial, and from almost anywhere in the world.

In the past, if you wanted to talk to someone in a provincial government office, you simply dialed the number. The receptionist would answer your call and direct you to the person you wanted to talk to. If that person wasn't in the office, the receptionist would take down a message and give it to that person when they returned, and they could phone you back.

However, this has all changed. A few years ago someone, who probably thought they were contributing to the advancement of the telephone, introduced the invention called voice mail. At the time the inventor probably thought he or she was doing a good thing. In fact, what they introduced was the death of telephone communications as we knew it.

Nowadays, if you want to get hold of someone in a provincial government office you dial a number and many things can happen.

First, you can be put into a telephone directory where the cold voice of a computer lists a number of confusing options.

You are instructed to pick one of the options and press the corresponding number. If you miss one of the options, you have to wait until they are repeated. If the list of options doesn't include your question or concern, you have the option of blindly hitting a number and pleading your case with anyone who may answer.

Second, if you're lucky enough to reach the right person but they aren't at their phone or are on the phone, you're thrown into the voice mail system again. You're left with a choice of leaving a message that may never be answered or hanging up and calling again.

These are just two of the examples that I'm sure a number of legislators and their constituents are familiar with. The voice mail system is not designed to benefit the caller. It is designed to benefit the end user.

Let me just say that I am not totally against voice mail. I do use it after hours in my office. But during the day people deserve to speak to a human being. This is a policy in my office.

The resolution I have put forward is a lot different than my original resolution. The original draft was watered down so much that those who know me may have thought I was losing my touch. I have therefore decided to include the meat of my resolution in the form of another of the 20th century's greatest inventions, a top 10 list. Therefore, it is my pleasure to introduce Bill Murdoch's top 10 reasons why the provincial government should pull the plug on voice mail:

(10) Rural and northern Ontario residents get whacked with long-distance charges every time they call Queen's Park. That's not fair.

(9) Voice mail promotes laziness. Even the most dedicated provincial employee is tempted to let a caller disappear into the voice mail abyss.

(8) If you are calling from a pay phone and get a voice mail you can kiss your quarter goodbye.

(7) After reports of my intention to recommend scrapping voice mail from all provincial government phones, my office was flooded with calls of support, all of which were politely answered by my staff and not a machine.

(6) A phone call to a provincial government office is a call to action, not a voice audition.

(5) Voice mail will change the course of history. Stevie Wonder will have to change the name of his Valentine's favourite to "I just called to say I love you, but I got your voice mail so we're through." Viewers will be outraged when Steven Spielberg's re-releases *ET* because the poor little fellow phones home and gets voice mail, leaving him on earth to be dissected by evil scientists.

(4) If you have enough patience to listen to the message and press the right button, you may be told, "Sorry, mailbox full, please call again later."

(3) It's a big, fat waste of money. We will still have receptionists to answer the phone when callers hit zero.

(2) In the Common Sense Revolution the government promised practical ideas for making the government work better for the people it serves. Getting rid of voice mail would be a step in the right direction.

And the number one reason why the provincial government should pull the plug on voice mail: (1) The taxpayers of Ontario pay the salaries of all provincial civil servants, elected officials and their staff and therefore deserve to talk to a living, breathing human being when phoning a government office and not a machine.

For these reasons and many others, I'm strongly urging the House to support the removal of voice mail from every provincial government telephone paid for by the taxpayers of Ontario. The taxpayers are our customers and it's our job to listen. I don't know how anybody could disagree with this simple concept.

Voicemail should be left behind on the scrap heap of useless 20th-century inventions like the Rubik's cube, new Coke, and spray-on hair. This is not a political issue. It's a matter of common sense. Let's get rid of voice mail before it's too late.

As a young boy growing up in Grey County, I was taught that if someone was taking the time to ask you a question, it is only polite to answer them right away. This simple lesson should be applied to the telephone. If the phone rings, answer it. Don't hide behind the wall of voice mail.

I look forward to hearing from the rest of my colleagues in the House talking about this, but I see I still have three minutes and my notes have run out, so I can talk about why I'm so irritated. It's annoying and we don't need this voice mail. That's why we have receptionists. I don't believe there's a ministry in this House that doesn't have a receptionist working for them. As I said before, in my office we don't have voice mail. If you ring my office and all my staff are on the phones, it will bounce to the receptionist at northern development and mines. She will take a message and make sure that my people get the message and hope that they will phone.

Author's interjection—At the time of this speech, the advent of the "cell phone, cameras, and email" had not even made its appearance in "civilization."

CHAPTER 24

"He Shoots, He Scores"

The title of this chapter is a saying made famous by the immortal Foster Hewitt, the original voice of *Hockey Night in Canada*. If Foster was able to enter the Murdoch Chicken Coop and see all the autographed hockey sweaters that this man has, he would be overjoyed. Why would Foster Hewitt be overjoyed? It's a simple matter. If the Maverick was taking Foster Hewitt in to see the sweaters, he would not be showing him the number of Montreal sweaters first, even though they are his favourite. The Maverick would be clever enough to show this man—who was every inch a Maple Leafs fan—the complete set of sweaters that he has of the last team of Maple Leafs who won the Stanley Cup in 1967. Every one of the sweaters has the player's autograph except for Terry Sawchuck and Tim Horton, who both suffered untimely deaths many decades ago.

The next sweater that he would show would be the Kenora Thistles sweater that represents the smallest municipality that has ever won the Stanley Cup. The Kenora sweater is from the 1907 championship team.

Having completely captured Foster's curiosity, Bill would carry on showing many of the over eight hundred signed sweaters that are part of the collection. This would include sweaters from the NDP legislature team that Bill played on, the Ottawa Senators sweater that Bob Charelli, an MPP from Ottawa, gave to him with the autographs of all the premiers of Ontario who were still living.

There are sweaters from Jean Beliveau of the Canadiens, Alex Delvecchio of the Red Wings, Keith Primeau of the Flyers, and Frank

Mahovlich and Nathan Perrott, both from the Leafs. Then there are sweaters of local heroes—Les Binkley, who played goal for Pittsburgh, Dan Snyder, former captain of the Attack who played with Atlanta before his horrible death, and Paul MacDermid in his Washington and Hartford sweaters. All are signed by the players.

Dick Waugh of the *Sun Times* wrote an article about the sweaters. The following are a few excerpts from this column:

> Each sweater has a story. Bill called former NHL star Bert Olmstead, who he found in High River, Alta. "How did you get this number?" enquired Olmstead, who wondered if Harry Lumley was still alive.
>
> Frank Mahovlich was in Owen Sound at the invitation of the Arthritis Association. He brought a sweater for a draw and Bill won it. This was in 1999 and the beginning of the collection.
>
> How about this one. Fred Saskamoose played with the Chicago Blackhawks. He was the first native Canadian to play in the NHL, but after 11 games went back to Sandy Lake Reserve where he became the chief.
>
> Milan Marcette played in the minors, but when the Leafs won the cup in '67 he was called up and played in that series. He never got a point, but has a Stanley Cup ring.
>
> Remember the Stastny brothers? He has a sweater with autographs with Peter, Anton, and Marrian Stastny, who were with the Quebec Nordiques.
>
> There is Jack Stoddard, who played with the New York Rangers and put his name on a jersey in this collection. He played in Owen Sound with the Mercurys. Curtis Sanford, who played for the Owen Sound Platers, is there.
>
> How about Danny Lewicki, who took the NHL "C" form to court and won. But no teams in the NHL would ever hire him again. He is in the collection.[9]

CHAPTER 25

The Fifth and Final Interlude

The ultimate Maverick is the being known as "Jesus, the Christ". Israel was under the control of the Roman Empire. The leaders of Israel were allowed to carry on with Jewish affairs as long as they did not act contrary to the Roman laws.

Jesus didn't have any real problem with the Romans, although the rumour that He was the promised Messiah was something that the Romans were aware of.

Jesus often had run-ins with the Jewish political leaders. He ate foods that were contrary to Jewish law. He healed people on the Sabbath, again contrary to the strict laws of the religious leaders. These religious leaders were also concerned that Jesus might cause difficulty for them in their relationship with the Romans.

When the great crowds cheered Jesus as He entered Jerusalem on what has become known as Palm Sunday, the Jewish leaders became very concerned. Although the Roman leaders found no fault with this Jesus, the Jewish leaders insisted that He be crucified—and He was.

The Maverick was supposedly disposed of, but He is Jesus the Christ.

CHAPTER 26

Back to the Wilderness

John Tory was the new leader, although he was not an elected member of the Legislature. His story of election to the legislature is interesting.

His first adventure into politics came in 2003, when he finished as runner-up in Toronto's mayoral race. After winning the Ontario PC leadership in 2004, Tory won a 2005 by-election in the riding of Dufferin-Peel-Wellington-Grey. In 2007, he decided to run in his hometown Toronto riding of Don Valley West, where he lost to the Liberal incumbent, Education Minister Kathleen Wynne.

It took Tory another fifteen months to persuade one of his colleagues to give up a secure seat so he could again lead the party from the floor of the Legislature. The final by-election results show Liberal Rick Johnson winning the riding of Haliburton-Kawartha Lakes-Brock by nine hundred six votes. Tory drew 41 per cent of the vote to Johnson's nearly 44 per cent.

The sitting PC member, Laurie Scott, resigned so that Tory could seek the seat. Scott won the riding by close to ten thousand votes in the 2007 election. The sprawling central Ontario riding had been held by the Conservatives since 1994.

Ana Sajfert, Murdoch's Queens Park Legistlative Aide, wrote the following about the 2007 election:

> With John Tory as PC leader, the party collectively felt it had a sincere shot at winning the urban vote, which is significant to forming government. MPP Murdoch, who never shied away

from openly bashing Toronto, believed it too. But then the brain trust pitched a disastrous policy, promising to give public funding to faith-based private schools in Ontario. It didn't take a lot of door knocking to realize how vehemently opposed the electorate in Bruce and Grey was to this proposal. Murdoch first pleaded with Tory to denounce it, and when that didn't go over well, he publicly denounced the plan, promising that if it came before the Legislature for a vote, he would vote against it.[10]

It seems Tory misread Murdoch, characterizing his dissent as "a jack-in-the-box…where you wind the handle and you don't know where something's going to pop up with Bill." John Tory also said, "If you look up maverick in the dictionary, Murdoch's name is there." But he also misread the Ontario electorate's appetite for that policy, and the issue single-handedly sunk any hope of the PCs winning a majority on October 10, 2007. One of the casualties of the election was Tory, as previously mentioned, as he lost his personal election in Toronto to Kathleen Wynne.

The Maverick from Grey and the party leader were now at odds. Tory did not seem prepared to accept that the Maverick was correct in his assessment of Tory's proposed policy. Tory seemed inclined to blame Bill for the election results. One needs to remember, however, that Murdoch maintained his own seat with a comfortable majority.

During the next year, although the Maverick was prepared to let bygones be bygones, Tory appeared to do very little to repair their relationship. In the early fall of 2008, Murdoch suggested that Tory, who once again had no seat in the Legislature, should be looking for another job. This led to the Maverick's suspension from the Conservative caucus.

A news release published on September 12, 2008 covered the developing story. It quoted caucus chairman Frank Klees as saying that the decision to suspend Murdoch was made unanimously by caucus leadership:

"While our caucus has always provided forums for debate and differing opinion between colleagues, and will continue to do so, it is also united in its demand for mutual respect and regard for the best interests of our members and our party," he said. "Murdoch will be offered an opportunity to commit himself to conduct consistent with these standards." [11]

Murdoch stated that although he was aware of the decision, he was uncertain as to his status in the house. He claimed that if upon his return to the Legislature he found his seat in the corner, then he'd obviously be sitting as an Independent.

The news release chronicled Murdoch's history with the party, citing him as "a thorn in the party's side." His first conflict with Tory concerned the pledge to fund faith-based schools in Ontario. The current battle, calling for Tory's resignation, was clearly "the last straw." Murdoch believed that there were other caucus members who supported his call for a leadership vote, but he didn't know "whether they have the guts to do it publicly or not." The writer went on to discuss Murdoch's legacy of being an outsider:

> Murdoch, sixty-three, was first elected to the legislature in 1990, but was always considered an outsider. When he went public with his condemnation of the faith-based schools plan, Tory compared him to a 'Whack-A Mole' game at carnival midways, always popping up with something controversial to say.
> Murdoch was never invited into Cabinet by premiers Mike Harris or Ernie Eves, both of whom he outlasted when the eight-year Conservative government was defeated by Dalton McGuinty's Liberals in 2003.[12]

One of the problems of being a maverick is the territory that goes with it. The "political correct" seldom can appreciate when an out spoken maverick proves to be correct.

CHAPTER 27

"My People Need To Be Served"

On May 6, 2008, Murdoch presented a petition to the Legislature on behalf of the people of the Markdale area of his riding. It was a petition asking for their new hospital to be built.

Four years earlier, these people had been asked by the government to raise half of the $24,000,000 that was needed to build the hospital. In quick order, the $12,000,000 was raised, but the hospital was showing no sign of being built. The petition stated that the new hospital replacing the old hospital was the only major medical facility between Orangeville and Owen Sound.

The petition that Bill signed and endorsed to the legislature had been given to him by Donna Hutton, who had spent most of her adult life in the medical field. Among the signees of the petition were Chapman's Ice cream, who had donated $1,000,000, the Markdale branch of the Bank of Montreal, Dundalk Dairy Mart, and the Peek Thru My Window business found in Markdale's downtown business area.

It is now 2016. To date, a shovel has not been put in the ground for this hospital.

On the same day that this petition was presented, John O'Toole, the representative of the Richmond Hill area, presented a petition on behalf of some of his constituents asking the government not to remove the Lord's Prayer from the Legislature's daily opening. On a day that was supposed to have very little happening in the Legislature, the Liberals presented a bill dealing with this issue, and the bill passed.

The Maverick was not in the House at the time. It had caught him off guard, because he had a petition from the people of the Hanover area asking that the Lord's Prayer be kept. It had been forwarded to him by Betty McDuncan. The Maverick had not presented it, because the bill had not yet been presented. However, the Maverick felt that these people had taken the time to get the petition together, so he needed to present it, which he did.

As a follow up, he sent a letter to the *Post*, in Hanover, which was published on June 27, 2008. The letter described what had happened. The Maverick thanked the people who were involved with the petition for taking the time and effort to be concerned with this cause.

A major event for the people of rural Ontario is the International Ploughing Match. In the Murdoch "Chicken Coop," Bill has posters of each and every year's event since 1980. The ploughing match in 2008 was scheduled for the Meaford area.

As the Maverick was now suspended from the Conservative caucus, he was not allowed by Mr. Tory to ride in the caucus wagon in the big parade that is part of this event. Instead, the Maverick, in his own riding, rode on a fire truck behind the wagon. The response in Grey was a foregone conclusion. The caucus wagon with Mr. Tory was booed. The man in the fire truck was cheered.

Since 2006, Bill had been working to help the raw milk seller in Grey. It was and is illegal to sell raw milk, not even to a group of people who are willing to join an organization that supports the selling of this product.

The Maverick had presented a private member's bill in 2006 asking that there be a full study of raw milk. The Toronto dominated legislature easily defeated this bill.

In November of 2008, a group of four people, including Murdoch and fellow MPP Randy Hillier, were named the "Four Amigos at Queen's Park" as they attempted to raise the raw milk situation in the eyes of the public. The Amigos were not successful.

Mr. Murdoch has stated that he was able to use his time as an independent back bencher to work even more for the people of his riding. He would—and did—demand equal time, according to the rules of the legislature, to speak on any issue he desired. His independent status gave him this right. He was to have equal opportunity with the Liberals, Conservatives, and NDP.

CHAPTER 28

Back in the Caucus

Following his devastating loss in the by-election in the Haliburton Kawartha Lakes-Brock region, John Tory resigned as the leader. The interim leader, Bob Runciman, invited Bill to rejoin the caucus in April 2009. When a leadership convention was held, Tim Hudak emerged as the new party leader.

The issue of the Harmonized Tax came to the surface shortly after this. In April, the same month that he returned to the Conservative caucus, the Maverick launched a petition in Owen Sound against the proposed new tax. Above all else, Bill and the Conservatives wanted to have public hearings. They wished for some of these hearings to be held in rural Ontario. The McGuinty government refused.

The Maverick's Toronto legistlative aide, Ana, described what followed:

> McGuinty was steamrolling with the new Harmonized Sales Tax and MPP Murdoch was growing grumpier by the day.
>
> On December 4, 2009, Murdoch donned his kilt and headed into the Legislature with a prepared statement in hand: "As you know, this is St. Andrew's Day, and I know we all want to celebrate that," he told the Legislature. "The people of Bruce-Grey-Owen Sound elected me to represent them. I serve them, I listen to them, and I represent them. Sadly, many members across the aisle have chosen to serve the Premier rather than serve their constituents. He does not deserve that kind of support.

Our caucus believes that the families who will be forced to pay the Dalton McGuinty HST should be allowed to have their say before the tax is passed. Public hearings. It is a simple idea, but not for this Premier. This Premier chooses to hide. This Premier chooses to deny the public any opportunity to have their say.

Dalton McGuinty once said he believed in public hearings. Now he's shutting them down. Where I come from, we call that a cop-out. Where I come from, Dalton McGuinty is a liar.[13]

Under Section 6 of the Standing Orders, members are not allowed to use "abusive or insulting language of a nature likely to create disorder." So when Murdoch delivered this statement, the Speaker rose and asked him to withdraw.

When Murdoch refused, firing back "No, sir. I believe that is true, and I cannot withdraw that," the amicable and popular Speaker Steve Peters offered the member a second and third chance to withdraw, before being forced to call in the Sergeant-at-Arms to escort Murdoch out of the chamber.

But Murdoch stayed, while his party colleagues shouted and pounded their desks in support—a circus that left Speaker Peters visibly peeved, and compelled him to remind Murdoch that "if the Speaker determines that force is necessary to compel obedience, the member shall be suspended for the remainder of the session. I further want to remind the honourable member that the definition of the end of a session is at prorogation."

At one stage, the Conservative caucus surrounded Bill and Randy Hillier, who had joined Murdoch and who also was suspended, to protect them from being physically removed from the House. Eventually Mr. Peters ended the question period, because it could not carry on with the noise that Bill, Randy, and the Conservative caucus were creating. The two MPPs remained in the Legislature over night in order to be able to carry on their sit in the next day. Murdoch and Hillier then apologized to the Speaker and left the Legislature to begin their suspension. The Liberals with their majority easily passed the Harmonized Tax Bill.

Andrea Horwath, the leader of the NDP in Ontario who comes from the Hamilton area, accused the two MPPs of being childish in their action. She stated that by negotiation she was able to get six more hours of hearings on the bill. These six hours were an extension of the hearings in the Toronto area.

As the Maverick says: "She and many others missed the whole point of the sit in. The point was that no hearings were taking placed outside of the Toronto area."

The Maverick was doing what he felt that he was elected to do. He was there to represent the people who had elected him.

CHAPTER 29

"Thanks"

The Maverick continuously supported many fundraising events in his riding. He also participated as a worker on numerous occasions. The following are but a few examples of this support.

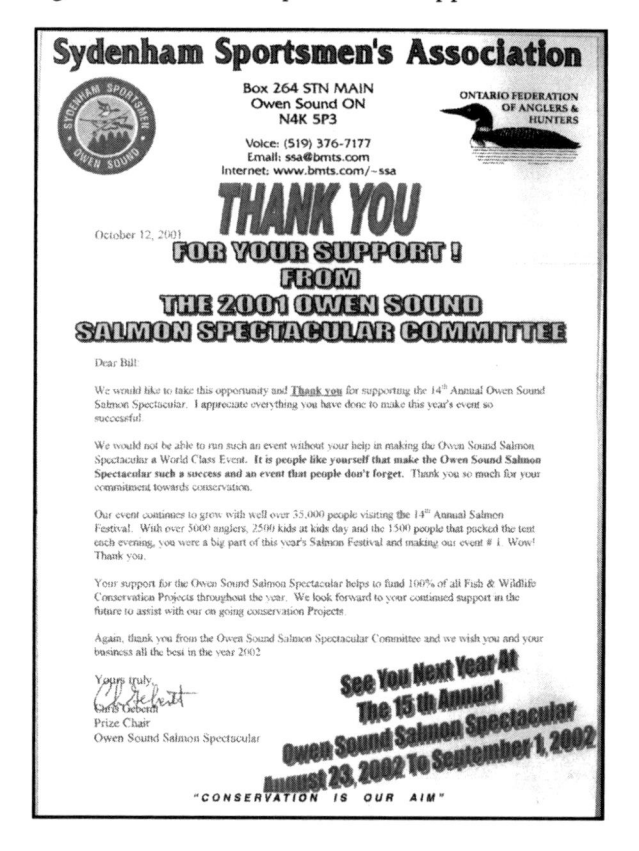

Sydenham Sportsmen's Association

Box 264 STN MAIN
Owen Sound ON
N4K 5P3

Voice: (519) 376-7177
Email: ssa@bmts.com
Internet: www.bmts.com/~ssa

ONTARIO FEDERATION OF ANGLERS & HUNTERS

October 12, 2001

THANK YOU FOR YOUR SUPPORT! FROM THE 2001 OWEN SOUND SALMON SPECTACULAR COMMITTEE

Dear Bill:

We would like to take this opportunity and **Thank you** for supporting the 14th Annual Owen Sound Salmon Spectacular. I appreciate everything you have done to make this year's event so successful.

We would not be able to run such an event without your help in making the Owen Sound Salmon Spectacular a World Class Event. **It is people like yourself that make the Owen Sound Salmon Spectacular such a success and an event that people don't forget.** Thank you so much for your commitment towards conservation.

Our event continues to grow with well over 35,000 people visiting the 14th Annual Salmon Festival. With over 5000 anglers, 2500 kids at kids day and the 1500 people that packed the tent each evening, you were a big part of this year's Salmon Festival and making our event # 1. Wow! Thank you.

Your support for the Owen Sound Salmon Spectacular helps to fund 100% of all Fish & Wildlife Conservation Projects throughout the year. We look forward to your continued support in the future to assist with our on going conservation projects.

Again, thank you from the Owen Sound Salmon Spectacular Committee and we wish you and your business all the best in the year 2002.

Yours truly,

Chris Geberdt
Prize Chair
Owen Sound Salmon Spectacular

See You Next Year At The 15th Annual Owen Sound Salmon Spectacular August 23, 2002 To September 1, 2002

"CONSERVATION IS OUR AIM"

Crime Stoppers of Grey Bruce Inc.

Wishes to Express our Appreciation to

Bill Murdoch MPP

*"What we do for ourselves dies with us
but what we do for others lives on"*

Thank You for your Generous Support

Pauline Kerr, Chair   Crime Stoppers of Grey Bruce Inc.

A BIT OF COUNTRY II

With Sincere Appreciation

Bognor Jam Production and Promotion Company

CNIB — The Canadian National Institute for the Blind, Ontario Division

_____
CNIB District Manager

For Immediate Release
October 21, 2005

Murdoch Honoured by Big Brothers Big Sisters of Canada

Queen's Park – At a reception Wednesday night at Queen's Park, Bruce-Grey Owen Sound MPP Bill Murdoch was recognized for exceptional support and for making a profound difference to the Big Brothers Big Sisters agency in his riding.

Nominated by Big Brothers Big Sisters Hanover & District, their coordinator, Marg Wettlaufler said "He's always there to help us out and Bill knows and supports our cause." She went on to say that he has been participating in their "Bowl for Kid's Sake" for 5 years and is more than willing to sell 50/50 tickets or whatever it takes to help out.

For over 15 years Murdoch has been participating in the "Murdoch Challenge" for Big Brothers in Owen Sound, an annual fundraiser held in March each year. "My schedule doesn't allow for me to be a committed Big Brother so this is my way of supporting an organization that I believe benefits a lot of kids," said Murdoch.

Ron Pegg

Girl Guides of Canada / Guides du Canada

Certificate of Appreciation

Awarded to BILL MURDOCK M.P.P.
FOR YOUR HELP WITH OUR CITIZEN BADGE
THANK-YOU! 1st FLESHERTON GIRL GUIDES.

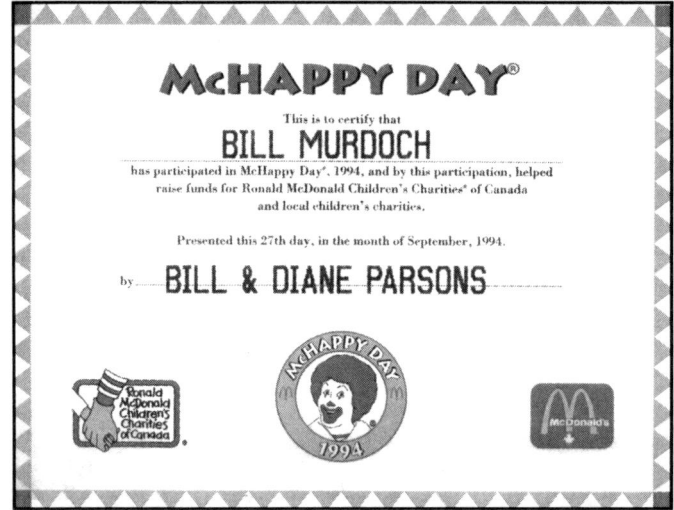

McHAPPY DAY®

This is to certify that

BILL MURDOCH

has participated in McHappy Day®, 1994, and by this participation, helped raise funds for Ronald McDonald Children's Charities® of Canada and local children's charities.

Presented this 27th day, in the month of September, 1994.

by **BILL & DIANE PARSONS**

LEGISLATIVE ASSEMBLY

BILL MURDOCH, MPP
Bruce–Grey–Owen Sound

August 3, 2001

Mr. Chris Peabody
Sacred Heart High School
450 Robinson Street
Walkerton, Ontario N0G 2V0

Dear Mr. ~~Peabody~~ CHRIS:

Enclosed please find photos for each of your students who visited Queen's Park earlier this year.

I would appreciate it greatly if you would see your students received this memento.

I enjoyed meeting the Students of Sacred Heart and look forward to meeting more classes in the future.

Sincerely yours,

Bill

Bill Murdoch, MPP
Bruce-Grey-Owen Sound
Encl.

Constituency Office: 1047 2nd Ave. East • Owen Sound • Ontario • N4K 2H8
Tel. (519) 371-2421 • Fax (519) 371-0953

Bognor Bill

Ron Pegg

Big Brothers of Owen Sound

P.O. Box 698
Owen Sound, Ontario N4K 5R
Phone: (519) 376-4449

Rec'd from QP   JUN 0 2 2003

May 26th, 2003

Bill Murdock
Bruce-Grey-Owen Sound
C/O Cory Shute
Room 270
Main Legislative Building
Queen's Park
Toronto, ON
M7A 1A8

Dear Bill:

On behalf of the Board of Big Brothers of Owen Sound, I want to thank you for generously contributing to our Bowl for Big Brothers Day 2003. You will be interested to know that the "Bill Murdock Bowling Challenge" was once again an important contributor to this year's record donation of $16,000. These funds go directly into our programs with Owen Sound youth now living in father absent homes.

I have enclosed a picture of a few of our rambunctious bunch, which is our way of thanking you for your continued support.

Sincerely,

Jim Belden
Member of the Board

c.c. Owen Sound Office

Bognor Bill

Fri, Dec 19, 1997

Dear Bill Murdoch,

Thank-you very much for making our turkey dinner such an overwhelming success. The staff and students of Meaford Community School appreciate your support.

Yours truly,
Students and Staff
of MCS

CHAPTER 30

Life After the Legislature

The Maverick continues to be the Maverick. His three day a week open line program on CFOS radio from Owen Sound is a forum in which people can call in and voice their comments on almost any issue. He has guests come to the show to talk about current events or causes that they represent. Past guests have included popular MPP Bill Walker, who was elected when the Maverick retired, and Larry Miller, the long time federal member in Ottawa. Both of these Conservative members continue, as the Maverick did, to represent the people who elected them.

The Maverick also has members of other political persuasions on the show. When one of them has written a book, or when Murdoch feels the person has something to say to his listeners, they are on the open line.

His broadcast frequently promotes local events and fundraising activities for charity. There are numerous people in the area who seldom miss one of the broadcasts.

Bill's passion for music inspired him to lead the way to the founding of the local music hall of fame. He still promotes concerts and musical events in the area. One of his recent gimmicks is to donate bottles of alcohol to silent auctions and other fundraising adventures. Bill doesn't drink alcohol, but he buys different kinds of alcohol to put into bottles that bear exotic labels such as Bognor Swamp Premium Whiskey—a thrill from the still.

With the ever-present twinkle in his eye, Bill actually has some people believing that there is a still in the Bognor Marsh where this alcohol is produced. It's all for fun in these day of the twenty-first century.

When the Ontario government changed its policy on who could perform civil marriages, the Maverick presented a bill about who could now perform these weddings. However, Mr. Hudak and the Maverick had a disagreement over this. As a result of this conflict, the Maverick's piece of future legislature died. The Liberals introduced a similar bill that passed. One of the Maverick's pastimes today is performing civil weddings, as he is licensed to marry people.

His long time County Council buddy, Murray Betts, has always liked to make his wife, Phyllis, part of his sense of humour. Although the Betts have been married well over fifty years, Murray told Bill that they had never been legally married, and he wondered if Bill would marry them. Bill said he would for a fee of $200. Meanwhile, Sue Murdoch said that she would sing at the wedding for free. Bill still has time for old friends as well as new acquaintances and future friends. Above all, he enjoys being with his wife and family, especially his granddaughter, Luella, at the ranch in East Upper Bognor.

CHAPTER 31

A Voice Crying in the Wilderness

It's not possible to end this book without mentioning the Maverick's final headline grabber in his last year in the Legislature. First, however, it's only fitting that the poem written by Jeanette Mazer of Durham become part of the manuscript:

"Vanishing Rights-County Restructuring"
Plans for County Restructuring are set,
What the Government wants, the Government gets
No one asks the little man,
Whether or not he wants the plan.
They keep on saying "this country's free"…
That's not the way it appears to be.
When taxpayer's rights in decision makin'
Out of his hands is constantly being taken;
And the bureaucrats decide forever more
What the taxpayer's dollars can be wasted for!
While his freedom of choice they relinquish and steal
The little man then is left to deal
With the unjust system of tyranny
Mistakenly called "democracy."
In a faraway country, in a foreign land
An oppressed people take a stand;
They fight for freedom in their life
With blood and tears…death, and strife;

> While we, here in The Land of the Free
> Give up our rights so easily…
> BUT, if there's to be such a thing as liberty
> In this farce that's known as democracy
> Then the little men must all unite
> And help each other sustain their rights
> Or the little man's rights will no longer exist
> There on the "Endangered Species" list! [14]

An article published in the *Sault Star* on March 11, 2010, covered another controversy stirred up by the Maverick:

> Bruce-Grey-Owen Sound MPP Bill Murdoch says it's time Toronto separates from the rest of Ontario.
> "The province is run totally by the mentality that is coming out of Toronto. The government of the day can't get anything done because they are overruled by Toronto," said the maverick MPP.
> The suggestion was sparked by a discussion at Saturday's roundtable in Chepstow among the Bruce County Federation of Agriculture and federal, provincial, and municipal politicians over Queen's Park's lack of understanding when it comes to dealing with coyotes in rural Ontario.
> Murdoch wants the government to broaden a program that pays a bounty on the animals, but says Toronto MPPs are horrified at the thought of killing wildlife of any kind.
> "Talk to the Toronto MPPs, they haven't got a clue as to what goes on up here. The majority of them come from the 416 area," he said. [15]

Murdoch suggested that the new province of Toronto would be limited to the 416 area code, but the 905 area code would stay within Ontario. He also suggested that the capital could be relocated to London. Although Toronto would still depend on Ontario for many of its "essentials," it would no longer hold influence over the smaller communities:

Murdoch said another example of a Toronto mentality imposing restrictions on rural lifestyle is the Niagara Escarpment Commission, set up more than twenty years to regulate development along the Niagara Escarpment.

Murdoch credits agriculture minister Carol Mitchell with understanding rural Ontario. She said on Saturday that after thirty years it's time that changes are made to the regulations relating to control of coyotes and other predators.

Tens of thousands of dollars of damages to livestock are caused each year by coyotes. Some critics of the government policy warn that the coyote numbers are growing and they are becoming emboldened and are showing up in urban areas. Some said it's only a matter of time before household pets and humans fall prey to coyote attacks.

But Murdoch warns that Mitchell too will run into the stone wall of the Toronto mentality if she pushed for changes that include killing coyotes."[16]

The Maverick's twenty one year career as the MPP for the area of Grey, Bruce, and Owen Sound had its foundation set in his first speech to the Legislature [Chapter 28]. There is no question that Mr. Murdoch was, and is, a maverick. He came from maverick country. Like most mavericks, he is consistent. Some want to call it bull headedness, or the lack of a desire for change, but regardless what one wishes to call it, in maverick Bill Murdoch— Bognor Bill—it is consistency at the highest level.

He went to Queen's Park to represent the people who elected him, and he did this to the very best that the present political situation would allow. His last years in the Legislature were very much years in the wilderness. The system would not allow the wishes of his people to be granted. He tried many different approaches, including his sit-in. Many are the people who do not understand, but many are the people who do not have this man's values and desires to serve his fellow human being.

The Toronto story is a star studded conclusion to an illustrious career. In 2016, the Toronto control of Ontario's provincial matters is staggering. Local municipal governments have virtually no control or power, even over most routine happenings in their constituents' lives. There are provincial regulations that establish the foundation of policy.

This Toronto control can be seen in sports, in education, in roads, in windmills, and other areas of provincial life. The Osprey area of the municipality of Grey Highlands had the right taken from them to register hockey teams in the Ontario Minor Hockey Association. The windmill issues have been taken almost entirely out of rural Ontario's control. Building laws and regulations often make no sense in rural Ontario. Grey Highlands Secondary School is a very different school than it was thirty years ago thanks to regulations for beyond the control of the people that the school serves. And again, the list goes on and on.

It could be that the Maverick's last hurrah in his time of serving his people was the most significant statement that he has made during his years of being a voice crying in the wilderness.

Fish Fry September '03

TimHudak &
Come Home to the Country
ONTARIO
PC
Celebrating
Rural Ontario

A Note from the Editor
Kerry (Doggart) Wilson

When I first picked up Ron's manuscript to edit, I was struck by his last name—Pegg. Memories of a childhood spent in the small town of Sharon, Ontario came flooding back. The name *Pegg* adorned many end-of-the-driveway mailboxes along the gravel roads of East Gwillimbury. Surely it was just a coincidence, right?

During one of our telephone conversations, I shared with Ron the memories his surname stirred up for me. Imagine how pleasantly surprised I was to discover that he hailed from the same line of Peggs as those in my hometown, and had even lived in the same area himself early in his marriage.

Ron and I had already discovered our shared love of history, and it was in this discussion that we also found out that we had both taught history in our younger years. My passion for history traces back to my high school days, when I spent countless hours learning under one of the best teachers I ever had—Lockie MacPherson. Mr. MacPherson inspired me to study history at the university level, leading me to an Honours B.A. in English and History from the University of Western Ontario.

Before I had shared any of these details with Ron, he mentioned that he'd been the head of the History department at a high school in Newmarket—Huron Heights Secondary School. What a serendipity to edit the book of an author who worked at my high school—albeit a decade before I arrived in 1981 as a grade nine student. All the same, Ron's impact on my life has been significant, for it was as head of the department in the late 1960s that he hired a young, new teacher to join the Huron Heights staff—Mr. Lockie MacPherson.

Congratulations on another fine book, Ron … and next time you see Mr. MacPherson, give him my love!

Endnotes

1. Patty Belle Sargent, *Roses in December: A Biography of Eddie Sargent* (Owen Sound: Ginger Press, 2008), 25.
2. Ibid., 26.
3. Ibid., 80.
4. Ibid.
5. Ibid., 93.
6. From the personal papers of Ana Sajfert. Reprinted with permission.
7. Ibid.
8. Dorothy Price and Dean Walley, *Never Give In! The Challenging Words of Winston Churchill* (Kansas City: Hallmark Cards Inc., 1967), v–vi.
9. Dick Waugh, *The Owen Sound Sun Times*.
10. From the personal papers of Ana Sajfert. Reprinted with permission.
11. "MPP Suspended for Suggesting John Tory Quit," *The Toronto Star*, September 12, 2008, accessed May 13, 2016, https://www.thestar.com/news/ontario/2008/09/12/mpp_suspended_for_suggesting_john_tory_quit.html.
12. Ibid.
13. From the personal papers of Ana Sajfert. Reprinted with permission.
14. Reprinted with permission.
15. "MPP Says Toronto Should Separate From Ontario," *The Sault Star*, March 16, 2010, accessed May 13, 2016, http://www.saultstar.com/2010/03/16/mpp-says-toronto-should-separate-from-ontario-2
16. Ibid.

Bibliography

Johnson, Ray. *The Bognor Chronicles.* Bloomington: Xlibris, 2013.

Pegg, Ron. *The Last of the Small Town Boys.* Belleville: Essence Publishing, 2005.

Pennington, Doris. *Agnes MacPhail: Reformer.* Toronto: Simon & Pierre, 1989.

Price, Dorothy and Walley, Dean. *Never Give In! The Challenging Words of Winston Churchill.*

Kansas City: Hallmark Cards Inc., 1967.

Sargent, Patty Belle. *Roses in December: A Biography of Eddie Sargent.* Owen Sound: Ginger Press, 2008.

Also by Ron Pegg

Trench Warrior
978-0884197805
Creation Books, 2001

It is said that one person can make a difference...but have you ever wondered if your life really counts? This testimony of one man's fight, his refusal to let his adversary overtake him and his trust in the orders of his Commanding Officer, will inspire and challenge you to let God use your life to accomplish great things for Him.

The Last of the Small Town Boys
978-1553069539
Essence Publishing, 2005

The rural village of southern Ontario where each person knew every other person, as well as each person's family history for at least three generations past, represents an era of history. Like *Anne of Green Gables*, *Tom Sawyer*, and *Sunshine Sketches of a Little Town* represent a time that is no more, *The Last of the Small-Town Boys* celebrates the passing of another time.

Cow Pasture Beginnings
978-1554520497
Essence Publishing, 2006

John McGraw, in 1913, stated:

"Naturally, I think baseball is the most admirable pastime in the world, a keen combination of wit, intelligence and muscle. It develops the mind, establishes discipline and gives to those who take part in it sound bodies, clear heads and a better sense of life" (The Old Ball Game, Frank Deford).

They Call Him Garney, I Call Him Dad
978-1-926676-12-8
Word Alive Press, 2009

Garney Pegg was the owner of a small town bakery and grocery in Beeton, Ontario for almost thirty years. The business began in the first year of the Great Depression and carried on through World War II and the 1950's. He and his wife Pearl raised a family of five while facing all of the problems that a small business faced in the hazardous time of the Depression and the War.

Giant Among Giants: Ernest C. Manning
978-1-926676-82-1
Word Alive Press, 2010

"After sixty years of having studied Ernest C. Manning and following his career, I firmly believe that the man who was elected in seven consecutive elections as Premier of Alberta, and who never faced a close election in his entire political career, a man who still can be heard on repeat broadcasts of Canada's National Bible Broadcast, is one of Canada's greatest people."

–Ron Pegg

Servant of the Shepherd King
978-1-77069-557-3
Word Alive Press, 2012

Can one servant make a difference?

"Ron Pegg has been a beacon of light for his family, friends, school, neighbors, church, various sorts and community. His love for God is obvious, and his love for humankind is expressed in his mission to the community and beyond. He has been a support and mentor to many people, including myself. You will enjoy reading about the life story of a man totally committed to his Lord and Savior."

—Marin Garniss
Providence, Manitoulin Island, Ontario
The Peggs' pastor

Tribute
978-1-77069-585-6
Word Alive Press, 2012

To God be the Glory! It was in the late 1970s when the Walls family and Frank Macintyre of the Dundalk Herald gave Ron Pegg the opportunity of writing a weekly column for the Flesherton Advance. During the next three decades he wrote the column under a number of different names. This book includes articles from that column, along with many recent works.

Here's Mrs. A: Canada's Woman of the 21st Century
978-1-4866-0500-2
Word Alive Press, 2014

Kate Aiken's young life experiences in Beeton were of the utmost importance in molding her into Canada's beloved "Mrs. A". Dubbed by her CFRB co-host Gordon Sinclair as the busiest woman in the world, she was a feminine dynamo who shared each of her experiences with her audience who loved her for what she was.

Ron Pegg
Box 213
Flesherton, ON N0C 1E0
(519) 924-3538
email: crpegg@bmts.com